KOREA, THE DIVIDED NATION

Praeger Security International Advisory Board

KOREA, THE DIVIDED NATION

Edward A. Olsen

PRAEGER SECURITY INTERNATIONAL
Westport, Connecticut • London

Library of Congress Cataloging-in-Publication Data

Olsen, Edward A.
Korea, the divided nation / Edward A. Olsen.
p. cm.
Includes bibliographical references and index.
ISBN 0-275-98307-2 (alk. paper)
1. Korea—History. 2. Korea (South)—History. 3. Korea (North)—History. 4. Korean reunification question (1945–) I. Title.
DS907.18.O47 2005
951.9—dc22 2005017481

British Library Cataloguing in Publication Data is available.

Library of Congress Catalog Card Number: 2005017481
ISBN: 0-275-98307-2

First published in 2005

Praeger Security International, 88 Post Road West, Westport, CT 06881
An imprint of Greenwood Publishing Group, Inc.
www.praeger.com

Printed in the United States of America

∞™

The paper used in this book complies with the Permanent Paper Standard issued by the National Information Standards Organization (Z39.48–1984).

10 9 8 7 6 5 4 3 2 1

Contents

CHAPTER 1

Introduction and the Geographical Setting

Korea is a nation and a land of considerable importance in Asia, and at times, in world affairs. Although many Americans who hear the word "Korea" primarily associate it with the Korean War, they frequently know little about either Korea, per se, or the major war that bears its name. Despite the controversy generated by periodic crises centered in Korea, especially North Korea, all too many Westerners remain unfamiliar with the basics of Korean affairs. Korea's location, its history of achievements and failures, and the ways in which Korea is perceived by its neighbors, the broader international community, and that community's leaders, has great significance.

Korea is often in the news because of international tensions, fears of conflict, and other contentious issues. For those who follow Korean affairs closely, keeping up with the nuances of such circumstances is not difficult. However, for many in the general public that is not feasible because they know little about Korea. This volume is intended to help fill that void. Although the conclusions drawn about resolving Korea's national division may be of interest to Korea experts as well, its general purpose is to provide those who are not experts on Korean affairs with a broad contextual background on Korea before its division, as a divided nation, and as a reunited nation-state. In that light, the selected references cited in this volume are intended to guide readers toward further readings on certain aspects of Korean affairs.[1]

In order to help readers appreciate Korea's importance, this volume shall describe and assess various facets of Korea. Following a survey of Korea's physical geography as part of this introductory section (chapter 1), an overview of Korea's traditional historical legacy is provided. Both factors influenced Korea's ability to cope with the pressures created by the advent of Western imperial intrusions in Asia and other Asian countries' adaptations to these geopolitical pressures, notably in China and Japan. The impact of that era upon Korea is examined by assessing Korea's colonial subjugation, postcolonial liberation, and post–World War II occupation division into the two Korean states that today dwell on the Korean peninsula. These initial portions (chapters 1–3) review the societal context for the emergence of a divided Korea and set the stage for the remainder of the volume, which focuses on the divided Korean nations' evolution and place in the international system.

The origins of the two Korean states and their respective political, economic, and strategic positions are examined. It is important to note a major fact that most readers probably do not know. Although the two Korean states on the peninsula receive a great deal of media attention, there is far more factual data available about noncommunist South Korea's domestic politics and economics than there is about its totalitarian communist neighbor, North Korea. North Korea is arguably the most secretive state on earth. Therefore much analysis of North Korean domestic affairs, including that found in this volume, must draw on limited data, reaching conclusions based on reading between the lines of North Korean propaganda, and inferential interpretations of comparisons to South Korea and to Korean history. In a similar vein, it is important to note in advance why the topic of Korean unification is treated separately from each Korea's foreign and defense policies, discussed in chapters 5 and 6. Although unification is touched on in these chapters, it is mainly addressed in chapters 8 and 9, after an assessment of each Korea's politics, economics, and foreign and defense policies (chapters 5 and 6), and after an assessment of the major powers' policies toward the two Koreas in chapter 7, because both Koreas treat the issue of reunification primarily as a theme to be addressed within the Korean nation—creating a context significantly separate from each Korea's international relationships.

Based on all these aspects of the two Koreas, a series of foreign appraisals of each Korea is provided in order to help the reader appreciate the importance ascribed to the Korean situation. Drawing on this background, this volume then moves on to assess how a divided Korean nation has attempted to resolve its differences, and examines how Korean unification is most likely to be accomplished. It concludes with an assessment of the impact a United Korea may have internally and externally.

Before moving on, an explanatory note regarding Korean personal and place-names is also necessary. Normally Korean personal names are used with the family name first, followed by a given name—usually a two-part name, but sometimes a one-part name. However, some Koreans, such as South Korea's first president, Syngman Rhee, prefer to use the Western word order and peculiar spelling rather than the standard Korean word order and spelling. In Rhee's case that would be: Yi Sung-man. This also is common for Korean authors writing in Western languages. Both styles are used here, depending on how the individual or the author noted has cited the name. Similarly, there are variations in Korean place-name spellings in English. The most frequently used versions, which are easier for Western readers to comprehend, shall be used here.

GEOGRAPHIC SETTING

For many non-Koreans who hear the words "Korean geography," virtually the only thing that comes to mind is the 38th parallel of latitude that symbolizes the division of North and South Korea. This latitude became famous after the Korean War as the proximate location of the post–Korean War Demilitarized Zone (DMZ), which divides the two Koreas and enjoys considerable geopolitical renown. As important as this factor is, there are other basic facts of Korea's geography with which those who are interested in Korea need to be familiar.

The Korean peninsula is located in Northeast Asia between the 43rd and 34th latitudes (north to south) and between the 124th and

131st longitudes (west to east). The entire peninsula is approximately 85,310 square miles, or roughly the size of the state of Minnesota. The peninsula is significantly smaller than neighboring China (704,000 square miles) and Japan (145,800 square miles). In its current politically divided configuration, North Korea is 47,130 square miles, or roughly the size of Mississippi, and South Korea is 38,180 square miles, or a little larger than Indiana. In terms of their populations, as of the year 2000, there were about 20 million North Koreans, although estimates vary widely due to the secrecy of North Korean society and the uncertain impact of North Korea's post–Cold War famines. South Korea's population as of 2002 was about 46 million. Their combined population is 66 million, compared to 127 million in Japan and 1.2 billion in China as of 2002. That means the combined population of the Korean nation is about half that of Japan and a little over 5 percent of China's. The latter ratio makes Korea similar to a substantial Chinese province. This sense of being overshadowed by its neighbors' larger size and populations gave rise to a Korean saying about being a shrimp between two whales and when the whales fight the shrimp suffers. While Korea's geographic context may have shrimp-like overtones, it is also important to recognize that the combined population of the Korean nation puts it on the same level as Britain, France, and Italy.

The peninsula is attached to the Asian continent, abutting the Manchurian region of northeast China and Russia's far eastern maritime province. The Yalu River divides the peninsula from China, and the Tumen River divides it from Russia. In Korean, the Yalu River is called the *Amnok-gang* and the Tumen River is called the *Tuman-gang*. Korea's ancient historical roots extend across these riverine borders, leaving a lasting legacy of ethnic kinship with indigenous people on the other side, as well as a sizable population of Korean migrants, especially in China. This causes some concern about Korean irredentism—a desire to reclaim territories with which they have historical ties—although it is unlikely to ever be acted upon.

The peninsula, or what Koreans refer to as a *bando* (literally *half an island*), is surrounded by water to the west, south, and east. Logically, Koreans refer to these as the West Sea (*Suh hae*), South Sea (*Nam hae*), and East Sea (*Dong hae*). However, most non-Koreans refer to the West Sea adjoining China's northern coast as the Yellow

Sea and call the East Sea dividing the peninsula from the Japanese archipelago, the Sea of Japan. The latter is a particularly sensitive issue among Koreans, North and South, who are adamant that the rest of the world also should call it the East Sea so that it does not imply Japanese control over that body of water.

Because of its half-island identity, the Korean peninsula has instilled among those who live along its coasts and on some of the over three thousand mostly small offshore islands, a long-term interest in fisheries. In historic times, Koreans also maintained a relatively significant maritime commerce as well as an interest in naval power when external circumstances called for it. As important as these coastal factors have been, Korea's socioeconomic roots have been much more focused on agriculture and land-based contacts with China. In that regard China's continentalism strongly influenced Korea's geographic mind-set. Although Korea has a significant maritime tradition, this tradition did not become as influential in shaping Korea's national identity as did a similar tradition for neighboring Japan. Not until Korea's post–World War II division, which carved the peninsula in half territorially and thereby denied South Korea land-based access to the continent, did a Korean state begin to consider itself a virtual island, dependent upon seaborne connections. Furthermore, South Korea's maritime and naval positions did not become a major factor in its geopolitical calculations until the Republic of Korea's (ROK) economy expanded sufficiently to permit South Korean leaders to pursue such goals in a credible fashion. Having achieved such economic stature, South Korea transformed itself into a serious player in maritime affairs and may well extend those capabilities to the entirety of a reunited Korean national state in the future.

The peninsula's location and geomorphology also has had a significant impact on its development throughout history. It is subject to the summer monsoon that carries moisture-laden air around the Eurasian continent from subtropical southern Asia. This tends to facilitate agricultural activities via heat and water in the growing season. This weather pattern contributes to Korea's hot and humid summer climate, especially in the southern sections of South Korea. The lesser known winter monsoon carries cold and relatively dry air out of Siberia, which sometimes picks up offshore moisture lending northern and central Korea a reputation for truly harsh winters. While these winters are often relatively dry because of the arid origins of the Siberian winds, when the winds swing over the East Sea and flow onshore, they pick up moisture and deposit snow on the peninsula. This is Korea's version of New England's nor'easter. Korea's cold winters and hot, sweaty summers left their imprint on many American soldiers who served in the Korean War. These soldiers then conveyed their memories—especially of the "frozen chosin" (at the *Chosin*, the Japanese pronunciation, or *Changjin* reservoir in north-central North Korea)—to many Americans at home about what Korea is like.

The peninsula's mountainous terrain—with a major mountain range, the *Taebaek* mountains, extending north-south roughly parallel to the peninsula's east coast, and the *Taebaek's* relatively significant offshoot, the *Sobaek* mountains, extending southwestward in the southern part of the peninsula, as well as numerous lesser mountains and plateaus—exerts a powerful influence on the climate. Korea also has a number of relatively—in worldwide terms—small rivers that flow within the peninsula. The best known are the *Han* and *Taedong* rivers that, respectively, traverse Seoul and Pyongyang, the capitals of South Korea and North Korea. Also well known are the two rivers that Korea shares with China and Russia, defining their borders, as noted above. While this terrain and its internal waters may not be impressive when compared to neighboring China, this setting has had a significant impact on the development of Korean society over the centuries. Koreans are very conscious, and proud, of their mountainous redoubts—especially the highest peak at Mt. *Paektu* (9,000 feet) and the scenic Mt. *Kumgang*, both in North Korea. As is true in parts of Europe and elsewhere, identification with one's home turf can contribute to significant linguistic and cultural subregionalism within an ethnic nation. This remains a prominent by-product of Korea's geography to date in each half of Korea and in the inter-Korean relationship.

The peninsula's location between China and Japan has had a huge impact on its history and on its regional role. The nature of this impact is aptly characterized by the saying about a Korean "shrimp." There is much truth in this metaphor as well as the perception of Korea being the vortex[2] of Sino-Japanese and Western imperial tensions. This truth is also reflected in the now-cliche insights that the Korean peninsula is the "land bridge to Asia" for Japanese aggression and the "dagger at the heart of Japan," endangering Japan from the Asian mainland. As perceptive as both these descriptions are, over the longer span of history the Korean peninsula has functioned as a cultural transmitter for Sinic civilization, which reshaped Korea and then spread via Korea into the Japanese islands in a more selective fashion. In short,[3] Korea's geographic configuration has not only helped define to Korea's cultural, economic, and geopolitical identity, it also has played a major role in transforming Japan, and influencing Chinese, Japanese, and Russian interactions over the territory and waters that occupy the space between them.

CHAPTER 2

The Legacy of Antiquity

Korean history is profoundly important to North and South Koreans, both in terms of their differing views of the complex time line that shaped their nation's role in Asia and in terms of the regional factors that yielded their national identity. Each facet of the legacy of antiquity for the Korean nation shall be examined in order to convey a sense of why Koreans are so attuned to their past's impact on the present.

Korean sensibility to history's legacy can be traced to several factors.[1] Foremost is their collective need to redress past wrongs inflicted by external powers, which accentuate Koreans' sense of aggrieved victimhood. This is most obvious regarding relatively recent history, namely their oppression under colonial Japan and their post–World War II division by the United States and the Soviet Union. More important for present purposes is the Korean nation's past relationships with various neighbors that have shaped its sense of nationhood. These relationships have contributed greatly to the evolution of Korean nationalism, which today influences how Koreans perceive their past and its impact on their national identity.

At the foundation of Korea's national identity is what may seem an oxymoronic question: how long has Korea been "Korean"?

Among Korean nationalists this can be an inflammatory question. According to one Korean legend, the first Korean state was founded in 2333 B.C. by *Tangun* (pronounced *Tan-gun*), who was the son of a deity called *Hwan-ung*. On earth, in a cave, lived a female tiger and a female bear who prayed to Hwan-ung in order to become human. Only the bear succeeded and became a woman who then mated with Hwan-ung when he led a band of followers to Paektu Mountain. Their son was Tangun, who founded a Korean state referred to as *Chosun* (Land of the Morning Calm). This founding myth, in varying formats, enjoys considerable popularity among contemporary Koreans, especially in North Korea, since Mt. Paektu is on its border with China and is supposed to have symbolic ties to the Kim Il-sung/Kim Jong-il father-and-son cohort that has ruled North Korea since its creation in 1948. That issue shall be explored further below, but in terms of the legacy of antiquity, the Tangun legend is important because of its ethnic themes and its contrast with yet another foundational legend. The second legend centers on a Chinese prince of the Shang dynasty named *Chi Tzu* (*Kija* in Korean), who supposedly founded Chosun in 1122 B.C. in southern Manchuria. This legend reflects early Chinese interactions with people living on the Korean peninsula, but also suggests Korea was a separate offshoot of Chinese civilization.

For obvious reasons Korean nationalists have not been as fond of the Chinese-linked legend as the divinity-linked legend. However, both are symbolic of early circumstances in the nation that came to be known as Korea. It is uncertain how far back in history extend roots which can be unequivocally determined as "Korean." From the perspective of the Tangun legend, those roots reach back to a mystical creationary stage. In these terms, this legend has parallels with biblical themes and with Japan's founding myth about divine origins stemming from a sun goddess (*Ameterasu Omikami*). In that supernatural sense, no one else has a claim on Korean territory being tied to an identifiably non-Korean ethnicity. The Kija legend does not offer that depth, but it does connote a clear separation from China—albeit with links that do not serve Korean nationalists' needs. As far as anthropological and archeological evidence suggest, both legends offer clues as to Korea's roots, but neither legend offers a definitive answer.

Human beings had lived on the Korean peninsula for many thousands of years prior to the legendary founding dates. Prehistoric societies probably date from the Neolithic (New Stone Age) era of about 5,000–6,000 B.C., but there is sketchier evidence of human activity in and near Korea for thousands of years prior to that. Even sketchier evidence suggests some human habitation on the peninsula as far back as the Paleolithic era. Given the sensitivity of Korean nationalists to claims of deep founding roots on the peninsula, the precise nature of this prehistoric era and how it made the transition into an era that can be unambiguously labeled "Korean" can be very controversial.

It matters greatly to these nationalists whether the peninsula became identifiably Korean because of decisive Korean-shaped events, or as a by-product of the spread of Chinese civilization along its borders. It also matters greatly whether the peninsula became "Korean" rapidly, either by settling vacant territory or by ousting its previous occupants, or by an incremental emergence of "Korean" identity through the assimilation of previous residents on the peninsula who could be perceived as non-Korean. Unfortunately for these nationalists, given the very long period of prehistory on the peninsula, it is likely that gradualism would characterize the manner in which the Korean peninsula became "Korean." The symbolism of the Tangun legend reinforces this view because the legend's tiger and bear metaphors suggest other early Asian groups. There were some of a Mongoloid heritage who used tigers in their shamanistic rituals, and other ethnic groups descended from paleo-Asiatic peoples (related to the Ainu of present-day Japan, a group sometimes classified as proto-Caucasoid) who used bears in their rituals—even though Korean archeology does not support evidence of bear worship there. As metaphors, however, the tiger and bear suggest an assimilative process yielded a Korean national identity.[2] Since that assimilation would entail a blending in Korea's formative stage of people from different racial backgrounds far enough in the distant past that the composite ethnic characteristics have become thoroughly diffused throughout the population, it constitutes a different model than the much less assimilative processes that occurred in neighboring Japan well after Korea's identity was firmly established. As a model the evolution that yielded a Korean identity may be closer to what produced a Chinese identity over many centuries of human migration and evolution. Precisely when the Chinese became "Chinese" is even murkier than defining Korean identity, but is equally as sensitive an issue among nationalistic Chinese. These comparisons are important for Korea because they are the basis for Koreans' ability to make a case for their ethnic identity being separate from their Chinese and Japanese neighbors. This strongly influenced the historical evolution of the entities that coalesced into a Korean nation state and carved out that state's relations with its neighbors.

Against the background of Koreans creating their ethnic identity, and their distinctive self-perceptions, Koreans proceeded to build a series of separate states that became the basis for an eventual nation-state. Although the importance of the Kija legend is primarily symbolic in terms of the factual chronology of Korean state-building, China's role in noting Korea's emergence was crucial. The early records of Korea's state-building efforts derive from Chinese scholarly and governmental sources. Korean histories of events do not become significant until Korean states became far more sophisticated and began to emulate the record-keeping of the established Chinese neighboring states.

The first notable example of these states was called *Chao-xian* (Morning Calm) by the Chinese, pronounced *Chosun* by the Koreans as they adapted Chinese ideographs for use in the Korean language. It dates to the third century B.C. and is commonly referred to today as Old Chosun (*Ko Chosun*), to distinguish it from Korea's final monarchical dynasty, the Yi dynasty, which also is known as the Chosun dynasty. The Old Chosun state probably encompassed portions of southern Manchuria and the northern Korean peninsula, but its precise realm is unclear as is its significance in its day. It was a Bronze Age civilization on the fringes of the Chinese empire in its formative phase. Factual evidence about Old Chosun is sparse. In many respects the empire's key significance is its role as a progenitor for successive states and the way later generations of Koreans revere its legacy and ascribe legendary links to the Chosun name.

The name "Chosun" is still used in the Korean language for "Korea" and is part of the formal name for contemporary North Korea—the Democratic People's Republic of Korea (*Chosun Minju Jui Inmin Konghwagook*). It also is widely used in South Korea. For example, one of South Korea's leading newspapers is the *Chosun Ilbo* (*Chosun Daily* or *Korea Daily*). In addition to referring to Korea as Chosun in contemporary Korean, the Korean nation also is referred as *Han*. South Koreans refer to their southern half as *Hangook* (the Korean country) or as *Dae Han Min Gook* (the Republic of Korea), call North Korea *Buk Han* (North Korea), and usually refer to the peninsula they share as the *Hangook bando* (Korean peninsula) but also use the phrase *Chosun bando*. As an indication of their parallel usage, another major South Korean newspaper is called the *Hangook Ilbo* (*Hangook Daily* or *Korea Daily*). The English name "Korea" seems to have evolved from other Western languages' pronunciation for a later Korean dynasty that will be covered below, the Koryo dynasty. The earliest reported English language use of "Korea" dates to 1614.[3]

In the wake of Old Chosun, the history of Korean states began to assume a more structured format. The earliest examples symbolize the ambiguous nature of the claims of Korean nationalists upon antiquity because of the ties of early states in Korea to events in China. Dynastic shifts in China that led to the emergence of the Chinese Han dynasty (206 B.C.–A.D. 200) affected Korea's evolution. Although a Korean leader named Wiman had established a state in the vicinity of today's Pyongyang early in the second century B.C. that built on the Old Chosun legacy, earning it the label "Wiman Chosun" among historians, the efforts of the Han dynasty to consolidate its power by securing China's borders led to its fall in 108 B.C. The Han dynasty created four outposts in Korea to control that portion of its border. These Chinese commanderies can be seen as an extension of China's provinces or as a form of colony. One of them proved more powerful than the others and lasted almost four centuries. The Chinese called it *Lolang*, but Koreans pronounced in *Nangnang*. Also centered in the vicinity of Pyongyang, it became a vehicle for the spread of Chinese culture into the Korean peninsula. It also became the focus of a number of Korean ministates, which were branches of the Han tribes located further south on the peninsula. It is important to note here that the Chinese ideograph for China's "Han" and for the Korean name for Korea, also "Han," differ. Over time, these states clustered into a federation that took the names Chin-han, Ma-han, and Pyon-han. They developed tributary ties with China's outpost in Korea that established a pattern adhered to by later Korean neighbors of more powerful dynasties in China. Of these, Ma-han and Chin-han gradually were transformed into a stronger state, Paekche, whose base of power expanded from the southwest of the peninsula toward the vicinity of present-day Seoul. Similarly, Pyon-han became the basis for the Shilla state in the east-southeast portion of the peninsula. Concurrently, but to the north of China's main outpost on the peninsula, two other states with Korean roots emerged. Centered well north of and in the Yalu river basin, the states of Puyo and Koguryo were created. Puyo's identity blurred the distinctions between Manchurians and Koreans, whereas Koguryo was more clearly Korean despite its territorial scope, which extended beyond the peninsula. Even though the evolution of these three states (Puyo is not counted because it's not completely Korean) was incremental and built on previous population centers, which can be characterized as tribal or clannish, each state had institutional turning points that permit most historians to ascribe them a founding year: Paekche in 18 B.C., Shilla (often spelled Silla) in 37 B.C., and Koguryo in 56 B.C.

Collectively, the history of these states is widely characterized as Korea's three kingdoms period. This period lasted until the creation of a unified Korean nation-state in A.D. 668, amalgamating these three separate states as well as other entities that nationalistic Koreans do not deem to have a truly Korean essence. Because this national integration process was central to the creation of a single Korean state that remained largely intact throughout the subsequent centuries under a succession of rulers, it was decisive in establishing Korea's identity. In that sense the national identity of each of these three kingdoms, which are so much a part of Korean history, should be considered as quasi-Korean en route to full-fledged Korean. The three kingdoms' relationships with each other and with China had a lasting impact on the Korean nation. Each of the kingdoms had relations with China that led to the percolating yet pervasive influence of Sinic civilization upon Korean society and its values. The perceptions of Chinese-invented Confucianism and Chinese-shaped Buddhism exerted, respectively, profound philosophical and religious pressure on Koreans. The major vehicle for transmitting this pressure was Korean recognition of the advanced stature of Chinese civilization, especially the merits of China's means of communication in writing via its ideographic characters. Although the Chinese and Korean spoken languages originally had little in common—Chinese dialects being multitonal, unlike Korean, which is probably an offshoot of the pan-Eurasian Altaic family of agglutinative languages—China's script and many of its words were adopted, then adapted, by Koreans. The many positive features of Chinese civilization were admired and emulated by Koreans in the three kingdoms. While much of this process symbolized Korean desires to show respect for and emulate their neighbors to the north and west, China's power and proximity also posed intermittent problems and opportunities for Koreans.

Because of its location, Koguryo had the advantage of easier access to China, but also confronted Chinese protection of its territory on their common border during periods when China enjoyed coherent powerful governments. In this sense, Koguryo became a geopolitical buffer for the entire peninsula, creating the military wherewithal to defend itself. During periods when China was inwardly less unified, notably after the fall of the Han dynasty in A.D. 220, Koguryo's need to defend itself was lessened, and its ability to interact constructively with Chinese on the other side of their shared border was enhanced. In this sense Koguryo was both a buffer and a conduit. Both facets of Koguryo had an impact on its Korean neighbors to the south. When Koguryo's relations with China and the two other Korean kingdoms were amicable, it served as a conduit or facilitator for greater Korean Sinification. However, when Koguryo's relations with its neighbors to the north and south were less than neighborly, the kingdoms' focus on Koguryo generated rationales for Chinese strategic cooperation with the other two Korean kingdoms. This rationale was underscored by periodic friction between the three Korean kingdoms predicated on their distinct identities and the tendency of the two southern kingdoms, Paekche and Shilla, to build external support systems designed to cope with the military capabilities developed by the northern Koguryo, mainly to deal with Chinese power. This complex of bilateral and triangular tension generated geopolitical forces that eventually led to unification of the Korean nation.

Curiously, these dynamics also contributed to the subnational regional identities of Koreans, with their roots drawing on the legacy of the three kingdoms and how each one's rivals perceived the others in terms of their cultural and societal importance relative to China. Those subnational identities contributed to parochial perceptions of each kingdom's relative stature that fostered a legacy of regional biases which persists into the contemporary era. That sense of cultural-political rivalry was initially most evident between Koguryo and Paekche, partly because of their relative proximity to areas of China—by land with northern China for Koguryo and by sea with more southern areas of China for Paekche. In time they became bitter adversaries in ways that evolved to Shilla's advantage. Prior to that, however, the kingdom of Shilla had to cope with what could be considered a fourth kingdom of the three kingdoms period—but is not treated as one partly because of its relatively small size but mostly because of its connections with the formative phase of Japan as a distinct entity. On the southern tip of the Korean peninsula, a small kingdom called *Kaya* by Koreans and *Mimana* by Japanese also was an offshoot of Korea's early subnational evolution. It was related as a clan cluster to the group that spawned the Paekche kingdom, but as a coastal maritime-oriented state also was a de facto conduit for Sino-Korean contacts with people dwelling in Japan. Since a considerable proportion of those living in Japan found their way there from mainland Asia via the Korean peninsula, the Kaya/Mimana people can be seen simultaneously as the last stages of a migration process and as a societal bridge between the peninsula and the offshore island chain. Despite its peninsular roots, Kaya/Mimana is today more identified with what became the Japanese nation-state. In important ways this perception by subsequent generations of Koreans, who cultivated their national identity by focusing on the Koreanness of the people in the three kingdoms, is ironic because a strong case can be made that all the peoples involved were part of an incremental transformative process that eventually yielded a Korean sense of national identity. In other words, it is difficult to make a case for the non-Koreanness of the Kaya/Mimana people when the surrounding three kingdoms did not fully warrant the encompassing pan-peninsula national label of "Korean."

Eventually hostilities between Shilla and Kaya/Mimana led to the latter's absorption within Shilla. This set the tone for what became the pattern of Shilla's expansionism. Events in China facilitated those developments. After the fall of the Han dynasty in A.D. 200, from then until the late 500s China experienced a succession of relatively short-lived kingdoms that struggled with each other from different centers in China to re-create a unified dynasty. Eventually the Sui dynasty succeeded in 581, although it only lasted until 618 when it was replaced by one of China's greatest regimes—the Tang dynasty. The Koguryo kingdom played a marginal yet important role in events in China. After the Sui dynasty established control within China, one of its priorities was to secure its borders from potential threats. Since the Koguryo kingdom was militarily strong and had expanded its domain from northern and central portions of the peninsula into large areas of Manchuria, the Sui dynasty attempted to exert its power by attacking Koguryo in 612. Koguryo had earlier in the mid-500s faced a joint Paekche-Shilla alliance against their northern rival. The alliance failed and caused major setbacks for Paekche, of which Shilla took advantage. In the wake of that experience, Shilla supported Sui against Koguryo. The main focus for Koguryo was to repel the Sui forces, and it inflicted a major reversal under the leadership of one of the most famous figures in Korean military history: Ulchi Mundok. Sui's defeat was catastrophic in scale, with hundreds of thousands killed, and it led to the dynasty's collapse. These developments sent profound signals to Shilla as well.

Although Koguryo was victorious, events in China spawned the Tang dynasty that refocused on dealing with Koguryo by developing a more coordinated alliance with Koguryo's southern rival, Shilla. This was not a new concept, because former Chinese states had cooperated with either Paekche or Shilla against Koguryo, albeit without success. In the process of strengthening that alliance in order to make Shilla a more effective partner against Koguryo, the Tang dynasty joined with Shilla in a two-front attack on Paekche that led to its defeat and absorption within an expanded Shilla kingdom. Given a history of periodic conflicts between Shilla and Paekche that had not forced Paekche to succumb to Shilla, it is evident that Tang's assistance tilted the balance in Shilla's favor. This had major consequences for Korea's future as a nation-state, but it also had a major impact on neighboring Japan. Since there had already been extensive interaction between Paekche and the people living in the Yamato region of the Japanese islands, who were in the process of creating what would become known as Japan, the defeat of Paekche provided an incentive for some of its elites to vote with their feet by leaving the peninsula and migrating overseas to Yamato, where they proved to be influential in shaping that culture.[4] A strengthened Shilla subsequently waged another two-front war allied with the Chinese Tang dynasty against their common adversary in Koguryo.

The defeat of the Koguryo kingdom in A.D. 668 marked the end of the three kingdoms era and the creation under Shilla of a unified Korean nation-state. This is symbolic in several ways that bequeathed a lasting legacy for subsequent states in Korea. As important as this merger under duress was as a symbol of Korean nationhood, the fact that it was precipitated by Chinese intervention and then shaped by post-conflict friction between the leaders of unified Shilla, who rejected the Tang dynasty's efforts to manipulate circumstances in Korea to its advantage, also left a lasting legacy for the Korean nation. The united Korean state, fostered by Chinese intervention, simultaneously gave the resulting unified Shilla reasons to be grateful for Chinese assistance but also caused Shilla to resist Tang meddling in Shilla's handling of the post-conflict situation in ways that led Shilla to expel Tang forces from Shilla-controlled territories. That mixture of gratitude and tension regarding their much larger and more powerful Chinese neighbor constituted a lasting legacy of ambivalence for subsequent regimes in Korea.

That ambivalence was underscored in ways that helped define Korea's territorial identity as one of being on a peninsula demarcated by the Yalu and Tumen rivers, when the Tang dynasty had to cope with a breakaway portion of the former Koguryo kingdom, called Palhae, located in the northernmost portion of the peninsula and a large portion of southern Manchuria. Even though Shilla became the Korean nation's first unified state, it was not totally in charge of everything on the peninsula that could be deemed Korean. The geopolitical relationships between Shilla and Palhae were strikingly similar to contemporary differences between North and South Korea in ways that may cause unease in Pyongyang because of the way Shilla eventually prevailed—at least within the confines of the majority of the peninsula. Palhae persisted as a viable northern variant that stayed beyond Shilla's control, but Palhae became preoccupied by ties with its Manchu neighbors to the north. Since the Tang dynasty also was concerned about the circumstances on its Manchurian borders, Tang-Shilla ties were reinforced because of shared interests vis-à-vis the Palhae-Manchurian connections. In time the southern portions of Palhae that were within the peninsula were absorbed into the Koryo dynasty that replaced Shilla, making Koryo arguably the first unified peninsular Korean nation-state. The remainder of Palhae, with its Korean roots, evolved in ways that integrated it into Manchuria's traditions. This proved to be important in establishing ties between the Korean people and their northern neighbors in Manchuria and Mongolia, who eventually became rulers in later externally imposed dynasties controlling China and, as such, perceived Koreans in a different light.

The net result of all this for unified Shilla was the creation of a relationship with the Tang dynasty that the Chinese considered tributary, but that the Koreans viewed as mutually supportive, enabling Shilla to benefit from being in China's extended orbit and to selectively borrow from Chinese traditions on Korean terms. In this sense, unified Shilla enjoyed a generally positive relationship with Tang rulers that reinforced distinctive Korean qualities. Because of the enthusiasm Koreans demonstrated for adapting Chinese culture to Shilla literary, religious, legal, and economic systems, it gained the respect of Chinese leaders, who rarely bestowed such compliments on China's neighbors—most of whom were scorned as uncivilized barbarians. During the Shilla dynasty's control of most of the peninsula, Koreans became devout practitioners of Buddhist beliefs, making Buddhism their national religion, and Koreans also became sophisticated advocates of Confucian philosophical guidelines in managing their society. Even though the Chinese perceived the Koreans as very closely adhering to a Chinese cultural model, the leaders of Shilla were confident that their emphasis on preserving the hereditary aristocratic roots of Korean extended family clans, whose feudal relationships skewed Korean approaches to Confucian doctrines, differentiated Korean society from Chinese society in positive ways. Shilla also created a distinctive identity by cultivating its maritime heritage, which not only enhanced its economy through a trading network but also developed a naval tradition that persisted into subsequent dynasties. In short, as much as Koreans acquired a reputation for trying to become more Chinese than the Chinese—in contrast to the more standoffish track records of the Japanese and Vietnamese—Korean self-perceptions did not fit that mold. Shilla Koreans were confident in their Koreanness and thereby established a pattern that proved to be both durable and a precedent for subsequent Korean traditional dynasties and later governments. One aspect of Shilla's history that reinforced Korean national pride in its diverse cultural and scientific accomplishments, centered in its capital city of Kyongju, was the way Shilla's reputation spread as far as South and Southwest Asia attracting visitors from Arabia and India who praised its stature.

Over time Shilla's advanced civilization became somewhat preoccupied with itself and inattentive to external and internal rivalries. Shilla's governing structure was based on what amounted to a balance-of-power system among major clans, which shared power intermittently. The tendency of these clans toward favoritism devolved into systemic corruption. Confucian principles were intended to cope with such human frailties. Even in China, where those pragmatic principles were more rigorously applied, the record was inconsistent. This was often explained by Taoist teachings about the *yin-yang* principle of striking a balance between positive and negatives forces of nature.[5] The symbol used to portray yin-yang became very important to Koreans trying to deal with societal dynamics and it is used today at the center of the Republic of Korea's flag. For the Shilla dynasty, however, that degree of harmony proved to be illusive. Corruption, favoritism, and clan rivalries weakened Shilla and made it vulnerable to rivals located to the north of Shilla's core base of support in the southeast of the peninsula. At the same time as Shilla was deteriorating, the remnant northern state of Palhae was trying to cope with aggression by the Khitan nation of Manchuria to its north. That struggle led to the breakup of Palhae. Part of it was absorbed into Manchuria, as noted above, but the rest of it was subjected to the rising power of clans descended from Koguryo, which took advantage of Shilla's decline and Palhae's collapse. These Koguryo-related clans also had to cope with clans that tried to revive links to the former Paekche kingdom and was able to prevail over them. These aspiring leaders, who shared Palhae's links to Koguryo, modified the name Koguryo to Koryo and developed the means to challenge unified Shilla and then take over parts of Palhae. In the process of pulling all this together, these new leaders established the Koryo dynasty that ruled Korea from A.D. 918 to 1392. As noted previously, the Koryo dynasty became the source of the word most widely used in Western languages as the name of the peninsula: Korea.

While unified Shilla usually is credited with being the first dynasty to bring together the separate parts of Korea formerly ruled by the three kingdoms, and, as such, is the foundation for Korea's national identity as a state, Koryo also warrants attention in this regard. Because a segment of the former three kingdoms, the Palhae portion of Koguryo, remained outside the unified national entity, one can argue that Koryo's succession after Shilla actually brought all the pieces together in a truly unified fashion. Perhaps the best way of treating this delicate issue is to consider unified Shilla as the foundation for the Korean nation-state that enabled Koryo to build upon Shilla's traditions even as it expanded Korea territorially to include all of the peninsula as we know it today. As much as this succession could warrant treating Koryo as the more thoroughgoing unifier of the Korean nation-state, Koryo—unlike Shilla—proved unable to preserve its political control over the domain it established when it succumbed to Mongol invaders.

In the early Koryo era, the dynasty largely perpetuated the societal order created by Shilla, thereby generating a sense of continuity that helped to solidify the Korean national identity. However, Koryo also adapted those societal structures to its more northern cultural consciousness. This tended to reinforce the regionalization of local cultural perceptions among Koreans, in which northerners perceived themselves as more rugged because of their ability to prevail in less hospitable circumstances (a harsher climate, formidable terrain, and proximity to threats from the other side of the Yalu River), while seeing southerners as less rugged for having a softer life and being overly preoccupied with their cultural endeavors. Southerners, in turn, perceived northerners as crude and less civilized, while seeing themselves as the core of what made Korea great. Furthermore, such views in the south had subregional biases, depending on a given area's historical ties to Paekche or Shilla. This type of regionalism became entrenched in Korea as leaders from various regions evolved and remained a factor among Koreans coping with divisive twentieth- and twenty-first-century issues, often exacerbating those problems. For present purposes, however, it is important to note how the Koryo dynasty reinforced cultural regionalism as a source of friction within the Korean nation.

In its formative years, the Koryo dynasty had to cope with northern aggression from the Liao dynasty of the Manchurian Khitan nation, which threatened both China and Korea. With its capital in Kaesong (just north of the present day Demilitarized Zone, or DMZ, that divides North and South Korea), Koryo also created a northwestern administrative center in Pyongyang (near the capital of the old Koguryo kingdom), and a southern capital, Namkyung, that evolved into present-day Seoul. The northern capital reinforced its roots in the past, but also left a legacy for northern Koreans that is drawn upon by present-day leaders in North Korea. The Koryo dynasty eventually prevailed over the Liao, but the struggle left a preoccupation with national defense and maintaining a society capable of sustaining it. The social hierarchy became more structured, with its civilian and military sectors drawing on past aristocratic patterns with feudal overtones. The elites became known as the *yangban*, a social order that became entrenched over time and strongly influenced Koreans under later regimes and to the present day. This society produced many achievements in the literary and fine arts, earning it a reputation on a par with Shilla for advancing Korean civilization. Perhaps best known outside Korea are the invention of movable metal printing type in 1234 (two centuries ahead of Gutenberg, albeit without the latter's pervasive influence) and major artistic advances in a form of pottery called celadon. Koryo civilization regularly interacted with China's Sung dynasty, which had succeeded the Tang dynasty. Each advanced the level of Sino-Korean cultural interactions. Within Korea's heritage, however, probably the best-known product of Koryo-era culture was the first major history book about what the world now knows as Korea—namely the *Samguk sagi* (*History of the Three Kingdoms*). It was completed in 1145 by Kim Bu-shik, written in Chinese, and modeled on classical Chinese history books.

Despite the renown of these achievements and Koryo's harmonious balance of Confucian and Buddhist practices, which made Koryo much closer to a Chinese paradigm than Shilla had been, Koryo's preoccupation with defending its northern borders as well as its clan-based rivalries yielded a relatively militarized authoritarian state. Its concerted efforts to defend the nation ultimately proved unsuccessful. When the Mongols in 1231 unleashed a series of attacks on Korea's immediate neighbors to the north, on a divided China under a weakened Sung dynasty, and on Koryo—as part of a Mongolian expansion of power throughout much of Eurasia—the Koryo dynasty succumbed to these pressures, but in a manner that enabled Koryo for a while to maintain a residual outpost amidst the Mongolian-run Yuan empire, which was based in China and lasted from 1271 to 1368. After resisting the Mongol invaders, Koryo leaders created a small enclave on Kangwha Island near Seoul, which was protected by fortifications and naval power.

The latter was a major asset because the nomadic Mongolians were not prepared for a maritime assault. Koryo also accepted arrangements under duress with the Mongols to help them reach Japan via Korean ships. Although that Mongolian effort failed, and in the process created Japanese animosity regarding Korea's role in the assault, coupled with Japanese reverence for the divine winds (kamikaze) that blocked the seaborne attack, Koryo carved out a supportive role with the Mongols that enabled Koryo to preserve what temporarily amounted to a limited form of independence, but at a very high cost for Korean well being because of Mongolian persistence. By 1258 the Kangwha outpost's ability to resist deteriorated, leading to Korea's thorough absorption under Mongol control in a manner that sanctioned a nominal Koryo regime, which evolved through intermarriage with Mongol royalty into a Korean branch of the Mongol rulers of China under the Yuan. The integration of Koryo and Yuan was sufficiently thorough that when the Mongols' grip on China weakened, leading to the creation of the Ming dynasty, Koryo was unable to survive very long after the Mongols were eclipsed. Rival cliques under Koryo clashed over whether to remain loyal to the Mongols or to shift toward the emerging claimants to power in China. One of the Koryo generals tasked with supporting the Mongols recognized the futility of the notion and rejected the mission in ways that caused him to take the lead in creating a successor to the Koryo. His name was Yi Song-gye, the founder of the Yi dynasty in 1392, which lasted until the early twentieth century.

Significantly, the circumstances that shaped the creation of the Yi dynasty were caused by an external power's intervention in Chinese affairs in a manner that was echoed more than five centuries later by the meddling of other external powers in Chinese affairs that again caused Korea to change course. There was, however, a major difference in these two sets of circumstances in that the events that helped to foster the transition from Koryo to Yi embodied a reassertion of centralized Chinese power under the Ming dynasty (1368–1662), whereas the eventual decline of the Yi occurred in the shadow of a foreign-controlled (Manchurian) Yuan dynasty in China that was struggling with other foreign (Western) imperial pressures. During the Yi dynasty's five centuries of rule in Korea, the longest of any rulers in Korean history, it had a decisive influence on the Korean nation as the world came to know it in the twentieth and twenty-first centuries.

Having been traumatized by the events of the latter Koryo era, especially by the ways a militarized society bolstered by Buddhist sectarian fervor had not managed to preserve Korean independence, the founders of the Yi dynasty (also known as the Chosun dynasty) and their advisors sought to put Korea on a better track by drawing on neo-Confucian reformist doctrines. These almost puritanical interpretations of Confucian philosophy have their roots in the late Tang and Sung dynasties of China.[6] For Yi leaders, neo-Confucian civic values were means to create an orderly society that could address the issues raised by Buddhists regarding a higher power that should guide people toward proper behavior but without theistic sectarian divisions that could exacerbate societal tensions. In essence neo-Confucianism provided rules to shape human interactions in ways that help assure harmony and discipline. Building upon longstanding Korean aristocratic traditions, this new emphasis on Confucian reformism led to the creation of a distinctly Korean brand of neo-Confucianism that was centralized, very hierarchical in its factionalism, and authoritarian in the ways that it inculcated group loyalty, deference toward seniors, and a fairly rigid societal order.

This proved to be very beneficial to Korea's evolution as a society because it injected discipline and focus into human pursuits, which helped advance Korean scientific and economic affairs. Korea enjoyed major accomplishments in mathematics, agronomy, meteorology, and medicine. To facilitate these endeavors and advance literacy, under the guidance of arguably Korea's most famous king, King Sejong (1418–1450), scholars devised a scientifically based alphabet for writing Korean called *hangul*. Unfortunately, because of the prestige of Chinese ideographic characters among Korean literary elites, this phonetic alphabet was relatively neglected until the late nineteenth century, when Korean reformers—under Japanese influence—attempted to educate a broader spectrum of Korean society. Nonetheless, it was a major achievement.

As a result of these endeavors, Korea prospered under the Yi dynasty in its early years. But it also became inwardly focused and less attentive to external events than it should have been. A negative byproduct of the Yi dynasty's preoccupation with Confucian reforms stemmed in part from its desire to not slip into the militaristic patterns of its Koryo predecessor. This desire was helped by the very harmonious relations between Yi Korea and Ming China. In short, the needs of Koreans to maintain truly strong group defenses eroded, and that erosion was reinforced by Confucian teachings about the proper and very limited roles of military classes in a well-run society. This does not mean the Yi dynasty ignored its military. The military classes benefited from their scientific achievements in terms of creating improved weapons such as cannons and armored vessels. However, when coupled with the greater prestige assigned to nonmilitary sectors of Yi society, the result was to make Korea a place that did not pay sufficient attention to security and permitted it to become fairly complacent. This was reinforced by the Yi dynasty's hierarchicalism and rigidity, which was based on a high degree of confidence that an internal and external natural order infused with filial piety would prevail.

That sense of national and international order was severely tested for the Yi dynasty in the mid-1600s by two external developments—Japanese aggression toward Korea and the decline of the Ming dynasty because of Manchurian aggression. Korean contacts with

Japan had been relatively sporadic in the wake of Japan's being influenced in major ways by both China and Korea during its formative phase as a nation-state. Japan's subsequent history had been largely focused inward on its national development and the cultivation of its own variation of Sino-Korean culture, which was markedly militaristic and feudal. The Japanese flourishing emperor-centered system was somewhat distorted by the emergence of a parallel military government run by shoguns, beginning in the late twelfth century. The Japanese imperial line remained intact, albeit not in charge of the state, even as a succession of shoguns continued. Eventually the shogunate system broke down due to long-standing endemic rivalries getting out of control. This yielded a quest to reestablish a single military power base, during which regional military commanders (*daimyo*) tried to assemble coalitions capable of elevating such a commander to the apex of power. When Japan had a coherent single- or dual-track governing system, there were commercial and cultural contacts between people in Korea and Japan. However, as the shogunate system broke down, those positive contacts eroded, and for Koreans, Japan became mainly an annoying source of piracy. That threat was essentially an offshore phenomenon, taken seriously only by coastal Koreans. It was not a sufficiently serious threat to cause the Yi dynasty to focus its defenses in that direction.

All that changed for the worse when the second of Japan's so-called three unifiers (Oda Nobunaga, Toyotomi Hideyoshi, and Tokugawa Ieyasu) decided to strengthen his position as a claimant to national power against those refusing to join his coalition by acquiring mainland Asian assets through the use of force. Hideyoshi (he is usually referred to by his given name because by birth he originally lacked a family name) had visions of conquering China via Korea and using that wherewithal to compel his Japanese rivals to accept him as shogun. Although Hideyoshi's plans ultimately failed in ways that discredited his attempt to unify Japan under himself as shogun, opening the door for what became the long-lasting Tokugawa shogunate in Japan (1603–1867), his two invasions of Korea, which lasted from 1592–1598, proved to be disastrous for the Yi dynasty. The Yi dynasty's forces, joined later in the war by Ming forces, were able to repel Hideyoshi's assault—aided in a major way by an innovative Korean admiral, Yi Sun-shin, who used armored "turtle boats" to attack Japanese ships. However, the damage done to the Yi dynasty's population, infrastructure, economy, and ability to govern effectively was enormous. Making things worse, shortly after these events transpired, Manchurians to Korea's north launched their attack on the Ming dynasty and its already weakened Yi dynasty ally. The victory of the Manchurians over the Chinese yielded the Ching dynasty, launched in 1644, which was to last just slightly longer than the Yi dynasty. The former fell in 1911, while the latter fell in 1910.

The creation of the Ching dynasty put the Yi dynasty in a very awkward position. Although the Yi dynasty was able to reestablish formal relations with Tokugawa-run Japan by 1606, this proved to be minimally important because Japan's early interactions with Western powers led Japan to adopt in the 1630s policies that amounted to a limited form of isolationism. Japan restricted its commercial contacts to the Dutch, Chinese, and Koreans, and even these contacts were conducted under tight constraints. For practical purposes Korean contacts with Japan withered as the Yi dynasty tried to fashion policies to cope with the emergence of the Ching dynasty. The Yi ties to the Ching had very convoluted roots due to the way the Manchurians, who founded the Ching dynasty, shared roots with early Koreans. These shared roots led the subsequent Manchurian,[7] Khitan, and Chin states to have ambivalent relations with Koreans, whom they perceived as distant cousins whose Sinified culture warranted admiration, but whose attitudes toward their northern kin seemed condescendingly similar to Chinese arrogance toward people they deemed barbarians. Koreans also referred to these people as *oranke* (barbarians). The Chin, who were bent on toppling the Ming dynasty, sought assistance from the Yi dynasty, which was still struggling with the domestic impact of Hideyoshi's assaults and hoped the Ming could help in that process and therefore had no incentive to undermine its Confucian big brother. Complicated by factional differences within the Yi dynasty, Yi leaders sent ambivalent signals to Chin leaders, who responded with diplomatic overtures that were unsuccessful and led, in turn, to Manchurian attacks in 1627 on the Yi. These attacks were intended to temporarily resolve the situation to the south before waging war on the Ming that would eventually lead to the establishment of the

Ching dynasty in China. While the emerging Ching dynasty was still based in Manchuria, it again attacked the Yi dynasty in 1636–1637 to get it to accept a subordinate role under the Ching, which helped finesse the propriety of Ching control over China that began, as indicated above, in 1644.

In the wake of these developments, the Yi dynasty experienced a prolonged decline marked by economic erosion, political stagnation, and a failure of leaders to lead in an effective manner. In contrast to earlier dynasties' track records of coping with problems in a creative manner, the Yi dynasty displayed a tendency to cling to inept organizational and management styles. The key to this prolonged decline was the internecine factionalism that dominated the dynasty's inner circles, allowing them to become inward looking and inattentive toward the declining socioeconomic status of Koreans living in the hinterlands. Compared to the levels of sophistication and prosperity that characterized earlier Korean dynasties, the latter Yi era gradually devolved and deteriorated. As a result corruption spread, civil disorder erupted, and living conditions worsened. Given the concerted effort earlier in the Yi dynasty to cultivate neo-Confucian practices, and the successes they achieved, the latter Yi's decline can be seen as a by-product of neo-Confucian practitioners' ability to transform their philosophy into something too arcane and metaphysical to be of much practical use. During this latter period, Korea produced some renowned neo-Confucian scholars, but they tended to behave in ways that Western critics of academia often disdain as the ivory-tower syndrome—out of touch with reality.

Had external factors not intervened in Korea, the odds are that internal events would sooner or later have led to yet another dynastic cycle of change. The Yi dynasty's preoccupation with itself and with its subordinate role beneath Ching dynasty suzerainty, even as the Ching's Manchurian leaders were becoming thoroughly Sinified by their Chinese advisors and minions, put Korea firmly in the shadow of China under the Ching. However, China and the rest of Asia were beginning to have to adapt to the advent of Western imperial inroads. This external factor would soon shape Korea's destiny too, but the Yi dynasty throughout the late 1600s and 1700s had very little contact with Westerners, buffered as Korea was by China. On balance, therefore, this phase of the Yi dynasty helped to shape a relatively backward Korea that was ill-prepared to cope with the new challenges of the imperial age. As much as Korea's prior history bequeathed a legacy of major accomplishments to the Korean nation, which are reflected in the deep-seated pride evident in contemporary Korean nationalism, the latter stages of Korean antiquity put Korea in a poor position to cope with the international factors Korea was about to confront. The decidedly mixed results of that coping process, which are due to the vulnerabilities of the mid-to-late Yi dynasty, and shall be assessed in the next chapter, help to explain why, despite Korea's profound national pride in its past, the legacy of Korean antiquity does not always serve Korea well in terms of Korea's ability to deal with the challenges of modernization and Westernization.

CHAPTER 3

The Imperial Age

Koreans in the pre-Western era of the peninsula had a long history of dealing with imperialism, but only of the Chinese variety. Partly because Koreans had become so infused within China's notion of a Chinese "middle kingdom" containing subordinate states in its orbit—some close, some loose—Koreans had gained a deep appreciation of the nature of that system of international relations. In that sense, Korean leaders were very sophisticated about who they were and how their nation fit into the only world order with which they were familiar.

If Western intruders in Asia bent on expanding their eighteenth- and nineteenth-century version of imperialism had had to deal with the kind of truly cohesive Chinese imperial international order confronted by very early Western visitors, the Korean vision of Sinic imperialism would have served Koreans well. Unfortunately for the Koreans and their fate, that was not to be. The relatively feeble Yi dynasty of the late 1700s and early 1800s was living in what amounted to a fool's paradise because of the perceptions the Yi leaders and advisors had of the outside world and China's role in that world.

Korea's ability to grasp the nature of Western imperial inroads into Asia was significantly distorted by being filtered through a Chinese perspective on foreigners and by the ways that filter was compounded by the Manchurian-Chinese ambiguities of the Ching dynasty. China's interaction with those foreigners who had a cultural base well removed from China's neighborhood in Asia, has a long and complex history.[1] Because that history strongly shaped Korean understanding of the outside world, it is important to briefly summarize it. While Chinese society kept its supposedly barbarian nearby neighbors at bay, it developed commercial relationships via the Silk Road in Central Asia, which had two broad effects on China. It reinforced Chinese convictions that the outside world, which had another form of civilization, was naturally attracted to the material and philosophical merits of China's superior way of life. It also led to Chinese exposure to those other civilizations in ways that allowed some of their beliefs to be transmitted into China on a gradual basis, which permitted them to be Sinified as they were absorbed. By far the best example of that was the way Buddhism was incrementally transformed from a branch of Hinduism into a distinctive sect that became a separate religion as it migrated out of South Asia, through Central Asia, and through western China into the Han ethnic core of China. This can graphically be seen in the artistic portrayals of the Buddha in the course of this migration that show his evolution in physical appearance from South, to Central, to East Asia.

Yet another major example of Chinese interactions with advanced alien civilizations came about as a by-product of the Mongol Yuan dynasty's network of ties in the greater Mongolian empire's outposts in Central, West, and Southwest Asia. This network led to an expansion of Yuan China's international contacts beyond earlier, limited Tang and Sung dynasty contacts with southwestern Asian (the Near or Middle East) peoples of Persian, Arabian, and Jewish background as well as contacts with Europeans as they had to cope with Mongol inroads.[2] These Western contacts led to the arrival of early Catholic missionaries and commercial representatives. By far the most famous of the latter was Marco Polo, whose writings (*Travels of Marco Polo*) whetted Western appetites for further contacts with China. Chinese contacts with the West after the Yuan dynasty fell were initially less open, but China's population and wealth attracted missionaries to the Ming dynasty—including the famous Matteo Ricci. Such contacts persisted under the Ching dynasty as well, its Manchurian leaders being less averse to cultural relations with Westerners than many of the Chinese mandarins who advised the Ching rulers. The prevailing dynamic for early Chinese interactions with Westerners was a profound sense of cultural Sinocentrism reinforced by Western desires to make use of opportunities presented by China in terms of its wealth, sophistication, and market potential.

In short, during all of these interactions with people dwelling beyond the Sinic realm, China was able to deal with them largely on Chinese terms—even if Western Christians also focused on the enormous Chinese population as latent converts. In the early phase of Chinese contacts with Europeans, this paradigm was reinforced by the way European Christian emissaries tried to reach out to China on Chinese terms and convey their biblical message with Buddhist and Confucian metaphors that could be persuasive within Chinese culture.

Koreans, who had exposure to these long-term developments in China's relations with Middle Eastern and European civilizations, had no reason to question the logic of Chinese perceptions of the primacy of their own civilization and the power it wielded. Koreans, living in a society that embraced the truths the Chinese expressed so much confidence in, shared China's perceptions and were content to deal with China as both a buffer and a filter. In short, the Yi dynasty—plagued as it was with endemic problems—was not interested in breaking away from the mold. However, elements within the Yi dynasty's social structure were more disposed to be innovative. Korea was not part of the early missionary efforts focusing on East Asia. Because of its location on China's northeastern border, it was not on the overland or maritime routes Westerners used to get to China. Nonetheless, those missionary efforts eventually spilled over into Korea. Initially that occurred as a result of Korean tributary envoys from the Yi court to the Ching court who, having interacted with Westerners in Beijing, acted as carriers of Western ideas back to Korea in the latter eighteenth century. That process was expanded by Chinese converts to Christianity, who functioned as missionaries in Korea, as well as by Western missionaries.

These voices for Western values, albeit somewhat Sinified, and for the scientific and technological stature associated with these Westerners, found a receptive audience among certain sectors of Korean society. The fact that these values reached Korea through China made them more acceptable among Koreans. The Yi dynasty's societal backwardness during the eighteenth century had contributed to mounting social disorder that created incentives for reformers to take action. While many would-be reformers sought to foment change based on indigenous Korean principles, others proved to be more flexible. This openness to alternative means led to the development of a cluster of thinkers who expressed interest in Western ideas and became associated with a movement referred to as Western Studies (*Suh hak*). This group interacted with, and influenced, another cluster of reformers associated with the practical studies (*Sil hak*) movement within Confucianism, who were committed to making what had become a fairly arcane philosophy more salient to the problems of everyday life in the troubled Yi dynasty. The Yi leaders resisted such reforms in an authoritarian manner that was superficially effective, but that also served to drive reformers into a more low-profile role that amounted to a subversive function further weakening the dynasty's effectiveness. The Yi dynasty's reactions to these external influences also ended up driving Christian converts underground to escape repression. These developments were important in that they led the Yi dynasty to react in a manner that made it both less effective in coping with its stagnation and less prepared to cope with later waves of foreign pressures on Korea. The Yi dynasty's reactions also created precedents for later examples of Korean inept handling of crises they would confront due to external forces. On balance, Yi dynasty Korea was poorly positioned to understand the challenges Asia confronted as a result of the spread of Western imperialism and made its own situation worse by isolating itself further from these emerging trends—thereby earning the pejorative label, the "hermit kingdom."

The early decades of the nineteenth century perpetuated these trends in Korea. Most of the action related to imperial inroads in East Asia was occurring on either side of Korea. In part, this reflected much greater Western interest in China's potential and in

Japan as an offshore site usable for those Westerners focused on China. Also, the relatively long-term Western efforts to get an imperial foothold in China, coupled with the level of economic success Dutch representatives in Japan had enjoyed since the mid-1600s, added to Western desires to improve their access to both China and Japan. Korea did not receive nearly as much attention. This is not to suggest Westerners ignored Korea. There were intermittent efforts to break through Korea's attitude of indifference, which symbolized its reputation as a hermit kingdom, but Korean xenophobia was ingrained in the national self-confidence displayed by the majority of Koreans. Overtures by Western representatives that were similar to those made toward China were rejected, and occasional shipwrecked sailors were tolerated until they could depart. On balance, however, Korea did not receive nearly as much attention as its much larger neighbors. This level of relative Western disinterest was heightened by the negative image Korea had inadvertently transmitted to the outside world via Westerners in China and Japan, who did not acquire a particularly positive perception of Korea from either of its neighbors. In China's case this reflected Beijing's intent to keep Korea in China's orbit, and in Japan's case it reflected its cultural ambiguity regarding Koreans as well as its relatively poorer basis for knowing what was going on in Korea. This was reinforced by Korea's memories of the legacy of Hideyoshi's attacks, despite having had centuries of intermittent formal relations, which were required by Confucian guidelines for interstate contacts within the Sinocentric regional system.

Thus, as the Chinese were attempting to cope with expanded Western commercial and diplomatic pressures from the late 1790s to the early 1800s, which led to overt conflict in the Opium War of 1839–1842 and its aftermath of tensions and accommodation, the Koreans were tending to rely on China's self-serving interpretations of how the Ching dynasty was dealing with Western imperialism. In that sense the Korean hermit kingdom was content to live in a vacuum created by its confidence in, and deference to, China. Part of the blame for Korea's situation can be attributed to China's overweening influence on Korea, but most of the blame rests with the Yi dynasty's leaders who did not pay close attention to the facts surrounding China's problems. Similarly, Korea was sufficiently complacent regarding its place in China's shadows that it did not pay much attention to what was happening to its eastern neighbor, Japan.

After doing their best to discourage other Westerners, who hoped to expand upon the trade access of the Dutch, the Tokugawa shogunate had to deal with the pressures placed on Japanese leaders by the arrival in the spring of 1853 of a small U.S. squadron, under Commodore Matthew Perry. This visit unleashed an internal debate—influenced by what the Japanese leaders had heard about what happened to China—over how Japan should react to the Westerners. The debate was cut short by Perry's return visit in February 1854. This led to negotiations yielding the Treaty of Kanagawa, thereby starting a process that led to Japan being opened to various pressures from Western states that, unlike the United States, were unambiguously imperialist. Although the Japanese tried to resist, using traditional means, it soon became apparent to the people who would go on to create the Meiji restoration in 1868 that such means would not be capable of coping with Western power. This unleashed further reactions in Japan that proved susceptible to desires for pragmatic solutions, even if that meant the Japanese would have to learn to adapt to Western power on Western terms. The key to grasping what was occurring in Japan is that the Japanese were once again (as they had done centuries earlier) prepared to adapt to, rather than adopt, an external model, thereby displaying societal flexibility as they evolved to meet the challenges posed by Western imperial inroads. Japan's reactions initially were expedient, but they soon came to epitomize a practical response to a new international environment that stood in stark contrast to Korea's lack of a credible reaction to China's setbacks and failure to be as pragmatic as the Japanese proved to be. Korea also did not pay close attention to what was occurring in Japan until Japanese responses solidified in ways that put Japan on a course that the Yi dynasty discovered too late to be able to take effective measures.

The net result of these developments was to put Korea in the middle of two neighbors that were dealing with Western imperialism in a radically different manner—China by muddling through and fending off serious change while Japan experimented with incremental adjustments that would cumulatively constitute profound change. For better or worse, the Yi dynasty under the guidance of the Taewon-gun (Duke Taewon) who ran Korea from 1864–1873 in the absence of an adult monarch, and under the leadership of his son, who became what turned out to be its last monarch, King Kojong, relied on China as a model for coping with the looming Western challenges. While one can argue that Korean reliance on a Chinese paradigm had merits in terms of being consistent and in terms of the very long-run harmony between Korea and China, for the remainder of the nineteenth century and all of the twentieth century, it proved to be a poor choice. In many ways Korean reliance on a Sinocentric paradigm, when blended with Korean xenophobia, set up Korea to be victimized by international factors with which it was utterly unfamiliar. In these terms, Korea was unknowingly poised to confront a steep learning curve as it was compelled to engage in the imperial age contest for international power, and thereby to remove its external buffers, and to open Korea to foreign inroads. This process was exacerbated by the Korean peninsula's location between its traditional neighbors, China and Japan, which were being torn by conflicting pressures, and adjacent to the far eastern tip of the Czarist Russian empire to its north. The geopolitical dynamic that emerged from this truly fit the label "vortex."

Foreigners bent on opening up Korea to participate in the wider world were initially cautious about meddling with a key Chinese tributary state. In 1866 armed efforts by the French and the United States, with the success of the Perry mission to Japan in mind, ended in failure due to Korean resistance and the extreme tides of the West Sea, which grounded an armed U.S. merchant ship, the *General Sherman*, leading to the destruction of the ship and its crew. The United States reacted to this by preparing for a naval assault on what they knew to be an important island near Seoul, Kangwha-do, but the plan was not implemented until 1871. Korean resistance to this assault was costly in terms of Korean casualties, but Korean fervor caused the Americans to withdraw. Had other events not intervened, the odds are one or more Western country would have focused its energies on opening up Korea in a decisive manner that the Yi dynasty could not resist. However, Westerners were not the only ones casting their eyes upon a Korea made vulnerable by China's weakened position.

In Japan, leaders of the new Meiji government were experimenting with means to expand their international contacts as a way to learn lessons from the imperial powers that loomed so large in Asia. In 1869 and 1873 Japanese representatives, drawing upon the Tokugawa shogunate's record of low-key trading relations via the Tsushima daimyo (located in the strait between Korea and Japan) with merchants on the southern tip of Korea, made overtures to the Yi dynasty for expanded ties that could be mutually beneficial. Because the Tokugawa-Yi interactions had been relatively marginal for both, this did not provide a promising foundation for improved relations. Korea reacted negatively partly because the pressure came from Japan, but also because the Japanese described their Meiji emperor in terms equal to China's emperor, unlike words used by Koreans to refer to their king. When the Japanese began contemplating taking more serious actions against Korea, even as they began to focus more clearly on building up Japan so that it could take advantage of China's weaknesses in an imperial age dominated by Westerners with colonial ambitions, the Ching dynasty started to become more innovative in the advice it dispensed to the Yi dynasty. The Meiji state acted on its plans by launching a couple of serious attacks on Kangwha-do in 1875, which led to Chinese mediation that failed to resolve the issue but nudged the Koreans into signing a treaty, the Kangwha Treaty, with Japan in 1876. The treaty formalized the supposed equality between Japan and Korea and opened three ports in Korea (Pusan, Inchon, and Wonsan) for trade with Japan. It also allowed Japan to undermine China's international role as Korea's Confucian elder brother, strategically buffering Korea. Although this agreement started a process that contributed to Korea being opened up to Western imperial pressures, Japan at that stage in its modernization under Western geopolitical influences did not quite fill that bill. Nonetheless, this treaty exposed Korea to unexpected international pressures.

From China's perspective, the Western countries that were encroaching on its domain posed a variety of challenges. Most of these challenges were maritime-based, with Western representatives showing up on Chinese shores in ships from far away and pressing for coastal trade and access inland. Given China's continentalist traditions, even the naval losses of earlier wars that compelled it to make concessions, enter into unequal treaties, and develop a foreign affairs bureaucracy to deal with Westerners, did not undermine China's strategic essence or confidence in its ability to cope with these threats by tried and true means. The one Western power that posed a land-based challenge via its overland imperial expansion was Czarist Russia, which had incrementally seized vast territories from northern peoples that the Chinese had long deemed to be barbarians. For the Manchurian leaders of the Ching dynasty, however, Russian expansionism posed a far more central threat to their core territories. That mind-set strongly influenced Ching perceptions of the outside world, which shaped the guidance provided to the Yi dynasty. There was unease about Czarist ambitions and uncertainty about the intentions of the upstart Japanese who were adapting to Western ways. As a result of xenophobic conservative Korean reactions to growing Western pressure for expanded access to Korea, both China and Japan dispatched military forces to Korea, tasked with stabilizing an increasingly uncertain situation. Of the two deployments, China's forces were more in keeping with Korea's traditions. Japanese forces, despite their mission to help Korea deal with Western-induced instability, reminded some Koreans of the legacy of Hideyoshi. Both of these deployments reinforced Beijing's complex security concerns. Western imperial powers encroaching on China's coastal regions were less directly threatening than the Russians or the Japanese. Among the Western imperial powers, the United States, partly because of its stated non-imperial position drawing upon its post–revolutionary war traditions, and partly because of its location on the other side of the Pacific Ocean without any colonial outposts in Asia, seemed to be the most innocuous of the lot and the safest to deal with.

Against this backdrop, the Ching leaders encouraged the Yi leaders to cultivate ties with the United States as a way to get as good a diplomatic deal as was likely to be attainable from any of the Western powers, and then use those arrangements as a precedent for other diplomatic arrangements. The central point in this approach was to fashion benign relationships with a set of countries that would not prevent Korea from continuing its interdependence with China in ways that would help both Korea and China cope with the changing international dynamic. Although some Koreans opposed this plan and sought to retain the Yi dynasty's so-called hermit approach to external players, China's influenced prevailed. In May 1882, Commodore Robert Shufeldt, who—as part of that era's naval diplomacy symbolized by Commodore Perry's role in opening Japan—had been interested in a more active U.S. role in Korea in the wake of American setbacks in the late 1860s, signed a United States-Korea treaty in Inchon that was created with Chinese assistance. That treaty was instrumental in opening Korea to a broader range of relations with foreign countries as several countries paid more attention to Korean opportunities and pursued their own bilateral treaties with Korea as a result. In that sense, the Inchon Treaty was a turning point for Korea in international affairs.[3] Although decades later the United States-Korea treaty received considerable attention due to the ways U.S. policy toward Northeast Asia evolved and because it was Korea's first treaty with a Western country, at the time it was just the first in a rapid succession of Chinese-guided Korean treaties with Western states. Korean treaties with Great Britain and Germany followed in 1883. In 1884 Russia and Italy signed treaties with Korea, followed by France in 1886. In a sense, the Chinese-fostered process of expanding Korea's international relations was designed to put Korea in the same position as China, thereby solidifying their bond in ways that were intended to make Korea a more vital element in China's protective barrier.

Despite Beijing's intentions and the level of de facto cooperation it received from an array of Western states as they pursued their own interests vis-à-vis Korea, things did not work out as the Ching dynasty and its Korean supporters hoped they would. The attempt to open up Korea in a rather controlled manner rapidly deteriorated into a far from controlled situation. As the foreigners began the process of establishing a diplomatic and commercial presence in Korea, this reinforced already significant tensions within Korean society. While the more cautious elements in Korea endorsed the approach China led the Yi dynasty into, other Koreans who were dissatisfied with the backwardness of their socioeconomic conditions began to explore Korea's alternatives by looking to the foreign representatives in their midst and to the paradigms embodied by the countries from which they came. Although some Korean reformers were interested in Western examples and tried to cultivate connections, this process turned out to be hampered by Koreans' lack of familiarity with these societies, the great distances involved in gaining meaningful exposure, and the ways that many of those countries' representatives in Korea could not genuinely claim to represent a country that had significant interest in Korea. Only one Western country—Czarist Russia—did not fit that description, and even it took a while to generate an active state involvement in Korea. This is not to minimize the generic roles of Westerners in Korea at this stage. Western merchants and missionaries played a significant role, by inculcating a more diverse spectrum of ideas among Koreans. Americans were part of this group, laying the foundation for later decades, up through the mid-twentieth century, in which Americans on the scene in Korea were active participants in cultivating Korean aspirations for positive change, but lacked a cohesive U.S. government policy to support such activism. This is not to suggest that there was not domestic support for such endeavors within U.S. society; there was such support in the form of organizations that funded missionaries and created opportunities for Koreans to visit and study in the United States. In this setting, other Korean reformers seized upon another external paradigm for reform that seemed to make a lot more sense in terms of its institutional salience, cultural compatibility, and the readiness of some of its representatives to advocate cooperation in helping Koreans improve their lot—namely, Japan.

Some radically progressive Korean reformers who had taken advantage of the Korea-Japan treaty relationship, and of Japan's proximity to Korea, to visit and study in Japan, became impressed by the way the Japanese people and their Meiji government were successfully coping with international challenges by adapting Japan to Westernized ways of modernizing. In turn, they began to press for Korea to emulate, in its own context, the Japanese model of modernization, calling this effort Korea's quest for authentic independence. When the Yi dynasty establishment-oriented supporters resisted the advocates of such reforms, some of the most radical of the reformers with ties to the Japanese tried to stage a takeover of the government, but it failed when Yi supporters called on Chinese armed forces, already in Seoul as part of the Yi-Ching relationship, to block the attempted power grab and its covert Japanese support. Because the Japanese armed presence in Korea by that point was relatively small, mainly guards at the Japanese legation, China initially prevailed. After Japan dispatched more forces to Korea to demonstrate its willpower, Beijing and Tokyo entered into negotiations led by two prominent figures in China and Japan: Li Hung-chang (who played a decisive role in arranging Korea's treaties with the Western countries) and Ito Hirobumi (one of the leaders of the Meiji state). Together they negotiated the Tienchin Convention in 1885, which led to both China and Japan removing their armed forces from Korea and agreeing to notify each other before deploying them again.

Had that form of a Sino-Japanese balance of power been viable, Korea might have been able to devise its own internal solutions to foreign challenges. However, the period from the mid-1880s to the mid-1890s proved to be a traumatic one for Korea. As a by-product of a mixture of internal discontent and a variety of foreign models for structural reforms, Koreans became more assertive in exploring their options. Among those Korean elites disposed toward such reforms, some looked to Americans and Russians, but most admired what the Japanese were doing for themselves and how the Japanese were earning the respect of Western powers operating in Asia. On lower levels of Korean society, reaching out to the peasant masses, a Korean cult called the *Tong-hak* (Eastern Learning) movement, which began in the 1850s as an effort to emulate Chinese reformers, had evolved by the 1880s into an admixture of Confucian, Buddhist, and pseudo-Christian belief intended to foster Korean self-reliance and discredit flawed foreign paradigms. The more some Koreans gravitated toward a Japanese-style of reform for Korea, the more the Tong-hak followers became stridently anti-Japanese in their form of Korean nationalism. In the spring of 1884, the Tong-hak movement attempted to launch a revolution against the weak Yi dynasty. When the Yi dynasty's last monarch, King Kojong, and his more assertive wife, Queen Min, called on China's assistance to put down the upheaval, the Ching dynasty kept its word to Japan by informing Tokyo about what it was doing. In response, the Japanese also dispatched forces to Korea. In one sense, both China and Japan were keeping their commitments, but in another more salient sense both Beijing and Tokyo were taking advantage of the situation in Korea to further their own regional interests. Japanese actions revealed a serious misreading of Japanese capabilities and resolve by both China and Korea.

The Japanese seized the opportunity presented to them to end the Tong-hak rebellion in Korea and to send a signal to China about which of Korea's neighbors had enough clout to determine the course of events in Korea. As Sino-Japanese tensions escalated, it produced a broader conflict: the Sino-Japanese War of 1894–1895. The war was partially fought in Korea, but also at sea and in coastal areas of China. While China's defeat in that war was not total, partly due to the difficulty inherent in a Japanese ground campaign against China and partly because of Tokyo's reluctance to antagonize all the Western countries bent on expanding their interests in China, there was no doubt that China's defeat was a major setback for China's traditional role in Asia. Even more important, Japan's victory marked its ascendancy as a major power in Asia. Japan was the only Asian state to become competitive with Western countries by integrating itself into their international system. Still more important for Koreans who found themselves in the middle of all this, the collapse of the Sino-Japanese balance of power overarching the Korean peninsula removed China as the factor of stability upon which Koreans had relied for centuries and opened the door to far greater Japanese involvement in Korean affairs.

Had Koreans acquiesced docilely to Japan's emergent power, those Korean reformers who admired Japanese self-reforms might have been able to work out an amicable relationship that could have prevented what eventually happened to Korea. However, Queen Min, who favored China, resisted the efforts of pro-Japanese elements in the government in ways that antagonized some of Japan's representatives in Seoul. These representatives responded by attacking the Korean officials who opposed them, killing Queen Min in the process. In turn, this aroused Korean opposition to Japan's geopolitical interests in Korea and discredited many of the Koreans who had favored emulating Japanese reforms in Korea, creating new opportunities for other Korean reformers who viewed Czarist Russia in a favorable light. The net result was to damage Japan's ability to exert political influence over Korea, even as Japan's economic influence in Korea continued to grow and as Japan's overall regional stature expanded, including the creation of the Anglo-Japanese alliance by 1902. As much as the Koreans who tilted in favor of Czarist Russia were confident they were backing the right horse in an international contest being waged around Korea, they severely misjudged the implications of what the British referred to as the "Great Game" between the two Western empires encompassing Eurasia via southern maritime and northern land-based routes. Although it was not as obvious as the Sino-Japanese contest for a controlling influence over Korea in the years prior to the Sino-Japanese War, something similar began to evolve between Japan and Czarist Russia. Because of the way Koreans reacted to Japan's ability to throw its weight around regarding Korea and because of the growing regional tensions between Japan and Russia, the Yi dynasty accepted Russian political advisors as a way to help Korea modernize with the assistance of Russian residents backed by their government—unlike the situation of a significant number of American residents who could not induce U.S. government support for an entrepreneurial role in Korea. Overshadowing this situation was a de facto agreement between Japan and Russia to create territorial zones of influence in southern and northern Korea, which many observers of the post–World War II situation looked back upon as a precedent for Korea's national division into the states that now exist. As symbolically important as that spatial arrangement was, in reality Korea was tilting further toward Czarist Russia politically, even as Japan's geopolitical ambitions were mounting in ways that were reinforced by its economic stature in Korea.

The Japanese quest for the Anglo-Japanese alliance was clearly motivated by a desire to buffer Japan from Russian pressures and Russian strategic arrangements with a vulnerable China that was inching toward its own internal collapse. Whether the Japanese intended to use that alliance as a stepping-stone for military actions against Russia in the short term is unclear, however, because Tokyo seemed to be intentionally biding its time until Japan was prepared to take action. When Russia in 1903 rejected a formal arrangement for Russo-Japanese zones of influence wherein the Japanese and the Russians would have acknowledged their respective influence in

Korea and Manchuria, which would have been a partial setback for Russia, their rivalry intensified in ways that was bolstered by the 1902 Anglo-Japanese alliance. In order to deter the Japanese from pushing such an agenda, the Russians tried to further expand their involvement in Korea to send a signal to Tokyo about who really mattered in the region. In the years since the Sino-Japanese War, two things had been increasing in Japan: Japan's military capabilities, and Japan's frustration that—despite major Japanese accomplishments—they still had not been fully accepted as peers within the Western imperial circle of power. The situation in Korea underscored this for the Japanese in that the Russians were politically benefiting from Japan's removal of Chinese influence over the Yi dynasty and were expanding upon that context in China in Manchuria. This went against the grain of Japan's confidence that its post–Sino-Japanese War rights in Korea and the economic stature that was built upon those rights were in danger of being undercut by Russian expansionism. In that setting the Japanese decided to take preemptive military action in 1904, which helped create a paradigm for what Japan would do in Pearl Harbor in 1941. In early February 1904, the Japanese broke off diplomatic relations with Russia, launched an attack on the Russian fleet, and then declared war. The Russo-Japanese War of 1904–1905 was part of a larger process in Asian international relations, but for Korea what mattered most was that it sealed Korea's fate for more than four decades. Although the war was mostly waged around Korea rather than in it, Korea was nonetheless a major victim of the war.

The Russo-Japanese War was arduous for Japan, but it emerged from the war with tremendously enhanced imperial stature, having defeated a major Western power and doing it in league with *the* major Western power—its British ally. The war ended via U.S.-sponsored negotiations, yielding the September 1905 Treaty of Portsmouth (New Hampshire), for which President Theodore Roosevelt won the Nobel Peace Prize. The treaty acknowledged an array of significant Japanese leasing rights in China, territorial gains in the Russian Far East, and—most important for Korea—Japan's paramount role on the Korean peninsula. Shortly after the treaty was signed, Japan started a diplomatic process with the Yi dynasty and exerted coercive pressures, backed by Japan's military preeminence, on its leaders. Korea had no viable alternative and signed a bilateral agreement in November 1905 that brought Korea under Japan's wing as a protectorate. For all practical purposes, this began the absorption of Korea into the Japanese empire. While a case can be made that in the initial phase of this protectorate, Japanese leaders intended to help backward Koreans improve their lot in life—a perception that was fairly widespread among Westerners until the Japanese empire became a threat to Western interests—after the defeat of Japan in World War II and to the present day, such views of Japan's role in Korea became discredited. Nonetheless, in the context of such early views of Japan's purposes, the continued Korean resistance in the form of reaching out to the international community for support proved to be counterproductive in terms of Japan's reactions.

The Yi dynasty, in what turned out to be its last attempt to preserve Korean independence, made use of innovative young Korean reformers affiliated with a group called the "Independence Club." The club started in 1896, after the Sino-Japanese War, and its members had contacts with sympathetic Westerners from several countries. One of these people was Syngman Rhee, who in the post–World War II era became South Korea's first president. Rhee had established contacts with Americans in Korea and was sent by King Kojong to the United States after the 1905 agreement to persuade President Roosevelt to put pressure on Japan. That effort failed because the United States, as part of its own imperialist expansionism after the Spanish-American War (1898), had reached an accord with Japan via the Taft-Katsura memorandum later in 1905, but before Syngman Rhee's arrival, an agreement with Japan that each would acknowledge the other's position in the Philippines and Korea, respectively. King Kojong also sent emissaries to an international peace conference in the Hague in 1907 that was intended to address disruptive issues in world affairs. That attempt also failed when Japanese pressure prevented the Korean delegation from being recognized by the conference as coming from a still-sovereign state. The shame of that event and other reverses within Korea caused some prominent Korean officials to commit suicide, events which hastened the decline of the Yi dynasty. Under further pressure from Japan, King Kojong stepped down, leaving the throne to his retarded son, who was a token instrument of Japanese officials.

Despite Japanese manipulation of this nominal head of state and Japanese installation of a Korean government under Japanese influence, Korean dissenters unleashed widespread actions against the Japanese, including an attempted assassination of the Korean prime minister installed by Japan. Japanese frustration was intensified when one of the Meiji government's most prominent figures, Ito Hirobumi, who had played a major role in shaping Japan's policy toward Korea, was assassinated in Manchuria in October 1909 by a Korean deemed to be a patriot by Koreans who opposed Japan's incremental takeover of Korea. In this cumulative context, Japan's top official in Korea, General Terauchi Masatake, pushed through a treaty that annexed Korea into the Japanese empire. It was signed on August 29, 1910, on behalf of Korea by Prime Minister Yi Wanyong, who had survived the assassination attempt the previous year. Yi was a pro-Japan modernizer who was used by the Japanese. Had history taken a different course, he may well have become a symbol of Korean adaptation to the Japanese way of reform. Instead Prime Minister Yi became one of the most despised figures in Korean history, widely perceived as a puppet of the Japanese and a traitor to the Korean cause. The 1910 treaty marked the end of the Yi dynasty and the beginning of thirty-five years of often harsh Japanese direct rule in Korea. It also marked the end of a single Korean government for the entire Korean nation—a situation which prevails into the twenty-first century. If today's two Korean states do not reunite into a single Korean nation-state prior to August 29, 2010, that date will denote for Koreans a legacy of one century without united sovereignty because of what Japan inflicted upon the Koreans when Korea was formally annexed by Japan.

The Japanese era in Korea's experience with the imperial age bears a much more complex legacy than just the loss of nation-state sovereignty.[4] If one compares the conventional wisdom regarding Japanese colonialism in Korea to that of Taiwan, especially based on the writings of post–World War II Koreans and Taiwanese, it is evident that they are perceived very differently. The prevailing view regarding Korea is that the Japanese were cruel, oppressive, exploitative, and bent on eliminating Korean national identity. Some such views exist regarding Taiwan, but usually they are toned down, less emotional, and far more willing to see the positive aspects of Japan's involvement in reshaping Taiwan by bringing it into the modern age as perceived by imperial powers. Generally, Japanese analyses of what Japan did in Korea and Taiwan after they were absorbed within Japan's Western-style empire is predicated on imperial Japan's intention to strengthen its position in world affairs by imposing Japan's brand of modernized organizations and its supporting values on people it viewed as materially backward. In essence the Japanese were doing in their colonial realm what Western imperialists did under the popular slogan "White Man's Burden."[5] As politically incorrect as that slogan is in the twenty-first century, at the time it was seen as a way to advocate benevolent humanitarianism through imperialism. For the Japanese of that time, who were being praised in the West for their sophisticated reforms and societal advances, their approach to imperialism was to help themselves by helping people they could bring within Japan's purview through exporting the Japanese way of life with all its material and cultural overtones. In effect, this amounted to an effort to Japanize these people for their own good whether they wanted it or not.

The reaction to such efforts among many of the residents of Taiwan, who had been somewhat on the margins of Chinese civilization, was much more receptive than among Koreans, who had enjoyed centuries of close relations with China and were confident that Korean culture and past achievements were virtually on a par with China's major accomplishments. Moreover, Koreans knew to their ethnic core that Korea's advanced civilization had been significantly responsible for the creation of Japan's early national identity. In short, the Japanese would never have become Japanese had it not been for their Korean roots. As a consequence, while many in Taiwan were open to the advantages to be gained under Japanese imperial tutelage, many Koreans were profoundly resistant to Japan's attempts to bear a Korean burden, even if it was for their own good. Moreover, those Koreans who had looked positively at Meiji Japan's experiments with Western-style modernization as a useful paradigm for Korean reforms were scorned because of the way their attitudes had facilitated Japan's incremental takeover of Korea. Such Korean attitudes conveyed to the Japanese an image that Koreans who resisted Tokyo's efforts were ingrates. The more such frictions appeared, the more the Japanese redoubled their efforts to push their cause in Korea.

As a consequence, Korea's experiences under Japanese guidance were a complex mixture of harsh cultural indoctrination, authoritarian political control, and rigorous socioeconomic transformation that left a major mark on Korea's development patterns as well as an ambiguous legacy of pride in coping with Japanese exploitation and bitterness toward the exploiters. Japan's approach to Korea after annexing it was to make it a well-organized and developed portion of an extended Japanese state. This was predicated on the form of capitalism developed by imperial nations to bolster their national wealth that is known as mercantilism. Although mercantilism has roots predating modern capitalism, its focus on using acquired assets to strengthen the home state blended well with Japanese hierarchical traditions. Central to this process was the economic logic of industrialization that the Japanese had absorbed from Western societies and the geopolitical logic inherent in the slogan *fukoku kyohei* (rich country, strong army) that was at the core of the Meiji state's quest for Western-style imperial stature. Japan had used both sets of logic for its internal development and building the basis for projecting military power. When Japan incorporated foreign lands within its purview, it applied the same approach to make use of these territories' assets for Japanese purposes. Based on what Japanese with experience in Korea understood about its climate, agricultural strengths, natural resource potentials, and human endowments, the Japanese empire made use of them in a manner designed to serve Japanese purposes.

To develop Korea to meet Japan's needs, the Japanese spread their bureaucracy throughout Korea to guide its colony along a developmental course that seemed natural to these officials. Most obvious was the agricultural potential of southern Korea's relatively rich lands and compatible climate, which are similar to Japan's best agricultural regions, but had not been well managed by the Yi dynasty. The great majority of the agricultural land was designated for intensive rice paddy use. The Japanese also incorporated into their colonial civil service as many well-educated Koreans as they could effectively use. To strengthen the prospects for building on these two elements, Japan's colonial overseers launched Japanese-style educational and institutional reforms designed to improve the potential of Koreans and their infrastructure. The more the Japanese learned about Korea's latent potential, the more they focused on the natural resources—especially iron and coal deposits—in northern Korea's mountainous areas, the northern rivers' hydroelectric energy potentials, the terrain patterns that suggested where roads, railways, and ports were most promising, and used all of these factors to create an industrial vision for developing northern regions of Korea and linking them to Japan via maritime routes. Similarly, they greatly improved the management of southern Korea's agricultural regions, enhanced the infrastructure of Korea's cities and towns, and modernized Korea's bureaucratic environment by bringing the colonial civil service up to the Meiji standards that had received considerable praise from Westerners.

Superficially these changes denoted serious progress in terms of Korean modernization, but—because all of these measures were undertaken for the sake of Japan rather than Korea—few Koreans perceive Japan's actions in a positive light. Most, conforming to conventional wisdom, describe Japan's policies in a very negative way, as the remainder of this chapter shall convey.[6] Although some Koreans were able to preserve their traditional approach to education, and others were able to participate in missionary-sponsored Western-style education, many Koreans who were educated under Japanese-imposed educational reforms received an education intended to Japanize them so they would conform to Japan's needs. Other Koreans on the lower end of the social order were mainly used for their labor within a Japanese-imposed system. Even though this approach acculturated these Koreans to Japan's modern work ethic, most Koreans view it as an example of exploitation and manipulation of Koreans forced to adhere to Japan's imperial mandate. Making matters worse was the cultural-religious overtone of Japan's imposition of its way of life on Koreans. Japan's representatives in Korea dealt with Koreans in Japanese, compelling those Koreans who wanted to do well to conform to Japanese language and cultural standards. Over time this led to pressure to use Japanese names when dealing with the Japanese. Japan's attempts to impose state

Shintoist beliefs in the divinity of Japan's emperor were perceived as undermining Korea's national identity. While many Koreans only paid lip service to such beliefs, and others, exposed to missionary activities, hastened the spread of a Christian alternative, they still saw such Japanese indoctrination as an effort to destroy Korea's national essence. Similarly, the Japanese imposition of their militarized brand of Confucianism tended to undercut Korean adherence to their nonmilitarized Confucian teachings and Japanized Korea's civil-military values in ways that had profound consequences for Koreans in more recent times. Such activities, and the stress on the Japanese language, have been widely perceived in the postcolonial era after World War II—when many people worldwide focused on Germany's holocaust activities—as an example of Japan's cultural genocide against the Korean people. While that may be overstating it, given the reality of Korean nationalism and resistance to Japan at home and abroad, there is not much doubt that had Japan prevailed in World War II, Koreans almost certainly would have been thoroughly deprived of their separate identity, transforming them into what would have become second-class Japanese.

As bad as such conditions were in Korea during the early decades of the colonial era, as time passed and circumstances in Korea and Japan changed, conditions grew worse. Part of the reason for this was the Korean resistance to change. Some of this resistance was internal foot-dragging. However, Koreans also actively organized to regain their independence from Japan. The most famous example of this was the March 1, 1919, nationwide pro-independence protests that the Japanese crushed. These protests were symbolically important to Koreans and are noted today by Koreans in both North and South Korea with a major holiday on March 1 (pronounced *Sam-il* in Korean). Some Koreans became activists in self-imposed exile as part of a provisional government for Korea based in Shanghai, but with representatives in other countries, including the United States where the Korean National Association established its headquarters in Los Angeles and supported the provisional government. Syngman Rhee was part of the U.S. organization. Other Koreans escaped from Korea to join the provisional government's volunteer army that was linked to the Nationalist-Party (*Kuo Min Tang*) government then in power in China. Others, bent on more active resistance to Japan's rule in Korea, escaped to help the Chinese communist forces or the Soviet Union's armed forces, both of which resisted imperialism in Asia. In the latter situation, North Korea's future leaders played a significant role. As important as all those developments were in shaping Korean views of Japan's role in Korea, they were intensified by internal developments in Japan. Although the formative stages of Japanese rule in Korea occurred under the purview of a relatively progressive series of Japanese leaders, from the late Meiji, Taisho, and early Showa periods of Japanese imperialism, and especially during the middle era's Taisho democracy, this did not mean these governments maintained a gentle policy vis-à-vis Korea. Moreover, as the 1930s unfolded, the Japanese government took a hard turn to the fascist right as militarists wielded power, putting Japan on the path to World War II. These mounting pressures on Japan to develop the means to impose its will with its Axis allies ended up exacerbating Japan's harsh rule in Korea. Because Japan relied on its assets in Korea virtually as much as it relied on its internal support network, Japan ended up maintaining a very large Japanese bureaucratic structure in Korea and deployed a large army contingent there to keep a lid on Korea but also as part of Japan's mainland Asian operations during the war.

The net result of all this was to intensify Japanese heavy-handedness in Korea and to generate Japanese demands for Korean labor in Japan and in Japanese-controlled Manchuria. As the Pacific War approached, the need for larger Japanese armed forces led to greater conscription of Koreans, especially into labor units. Relatively few Koreans were selected by the Japanese for responsible positions in the Japanese military, although some became officers educated under the Japanese military system. Most notable among the latter in later years was South Korea's General Park Chung Hee, who carried out a coup that eventually enabled him to become president. The combination of an intensified period of harsh Japanese rule in Korea at the juncture of imperial Japan's beginning of a geopolitical quest that would lead to its defeat, reinforced among Koreans the negativity of Japan's tenure as their colonial oppressor. Many Koreans see Japan's defeat in World War II as a form of payback for its harsh rule in Korea and think of Korea's resistance as a contributing factor in Japan's loss in the war. Korean conventional wisdom is very negative regarding the Japanese colonial era. Although a credible case can be made that postwar Korea's political-economic ability to cope with the modern world's challenges and the infrastructure that both postwar Korean states used to organize their governments owes a debt to the legacy of Japan-induced modernization, Koreans of all political stripes are overwhelmingly reluctant to acknowledge such a legacy and are very uncomfortable when non-Koreans discuss that legacy objectively.[7]

Koreans, especially in North Korea, like to emphasize the roles Koreans played in helping to bring about Japan's defeat in World War II. While some Koreans did help that process via subversive efforts within Korea to damage Japan's war-making capabilities, and still more Koreans performed military roles in the allied forces—especially in China and the Soviet Union, but also in the U.S. armed forces—their efforts were not decisive in Japan's defeat. It occurred primarily because of the massive attacks on Japan led by the United States. Nonetheless, Korean efforts were part of the support network, so it is legitimate for Koreans to claim some of the credit, albeit not the majority. This reality is crucial because of the impact Japan's defeat was to have on Korea as it coped with the end of the colonial era and the advent of a new era.

CHAPTER 4

Liberation and Division

August 15, 1945, was a momentous day for Korea. Japan's surrender to the United States and its allies symbolized for Korea its liberation from Japan. It is marked as a major holiday in both South and North Korea. However, the fact that the holiday is not celebrated in a single Korean nation-state graphically underscores the reality that Korea's liberation was not what Koreans truly wanted it to be. To get a sense of Korean expectations about the consequences of Japan's removal as Korea's oppressor, it is best to examine the planning that occurred during World War II with regard to Korea's future. Despite the high hopes of Koreans in self-imposed exile abroad—especially in China, the United States, and the Soviet Union—who aspired to be part of a would-be successor government, and those Koreans serving in the armed forces of allied countries—especially the significant numbers in the Soviet armed forces—who collectively symbolized Korean resistance to Japanese oppression, the track record of allied wartime planning regarding Korea was skimpy.

Largely because allied leaders had to treat all sectors of Japan's war machine as segments of a whole, and Korea constituted a significant part of that apparatus, the contingencies for dealing with a prospective post–World War II Korea had to be treated as a subset of dealing with a defeated Japan. In short, allied planners could hope that Korea would be easier to cope with than Japan, and that Koreans in Korea would respond in a manner ascribed to them by Koreans in exile, but they could not be certain that the postwar adjustment process would evolve in a predictably positive fashion. Moreover, these planners had no truly viable regime-in-waiting ready to install in Korea after Japanese colonialists were removed. Hence their contingency planning had to be kept flexible and adaptable. The net result was the pronouncement of allied leaders at the Cairo conference in 1943 of the famous (or infamous, depending upon one's perspective) "in due course" mandate. The United States, China, and Great Britain committed themselves to Korea's future in the Cairo declaration by stating, the "three powers, mindful of the enslavement of the people of Korea, are determined that in due course Korea shall become free and independent." Although the Soviet Union also was part of the allied coalition, it did not enter the war against Japan until very late and was not part of the Cairo session. On balance, however, its initial views regarding Korea's future, once it was removed from Japan's control, were virtually as ambivalent about the pace of full Korean liberation. In that sense, the "in due course" paradigm was applicable to all the external players with a national interest in Korea's postwar fate.[1]

A significant element in all these countries' contingency planning for Korea's liberation from Japan was the degree of uncertainty surrounding two international factors. It was unknown whether Koreans, having put up with Japanese colonialism for so many years and being in need of some external assistance, would be ready to accept such assistance from its two territorial neighbors—China and the Soviet Union—given Koreans' intense past experiences with the Chinese and Russians. That unknown was compounded by how the Koreans might perceive the United States, given its previous ambivalent experiences vis-à-vis Korea. This first factor was complicated by the second nuanced factor, namely the growing concerns about how to cope with an array of countries that would be rescued from Japan and how to deal with all these countries' postwar adjustment to the European and American colonial legacy in Asia. Effective criteria had to be developed for each of them, a task made more difficult by the very different world views of the United States, Great Britain, the Soviet Union, and China. As the eruption of Cold War friction demonstrated, that second factor proved to be salient.

After Japan's surrender and as Koreans began to cope with their international rescuers in ways that shall be examined here, Korean attitudes toward the countries of greatest concern became evident in an early postwar saying: "Do not trust the United States. Do not be deceived by the Soviet Union. Japan will rise again. Be careful, Korea" (in Korean: *Migook ul michi mal go. Soryun aegae sokji malla. Ilbon un iluh nanda. Chosun ah joshim haera*). This symbolic saying has to be perceived from Korea's context, based on prior experiences. In essence it meant the Koreans did not believe Americans could be relied upon to be consistent, feared the Russians would promise more than they could deliver, and were convinced Japan would someday pose yet another threat to Korea. As insightful as this saying was in the mid-1940s—and arguably remains in the twenty-first century—what is especially important is the absence of biting remarks about China. By implication China was given a pass by the Koreans. In that regard, it is important to recall China's nineteenth-century role in advising Korea on how to deal with Americans, Russians, and Japanese. A prominent official at the Chinese legation in Tokyo in 1880 urged the Yi dynasty to be wary of a Russian option by advising the Koreans "to become intimate with China, develop a friendly association with Japan, and conclude an alliance with the United States."[2] What this message conveyed to the Koreans was the need to rely on China, deal with Japan as much as necessary, and create relations with the most malleable Western power, the United States. Clearly, Koreans' experiences with Russia, the United States, and Japan transformed the way Koreans perceived each of these countries, and China, as they entered the post-liberation phase of their nation's evolution.

If Koreans of all political persuasions had possessed a crystal ball in early August 1945 capable of foretelling what was about to unfold internationally regarding the post–World War II destiny of Korea, in terms of the evolution of the Cold War and the eruption of an all-too-hot Korean War, there is no doubt they would have done far more to create a viable foundation for an independent Korean nation-state. With all of the advantages of well-informed hindsight, it is clear the potential leaders of such a Korean state could have coped with the situation bestowed upon them far better than they, in fact, did. Two questions must be addressed in that regard. What did these leaders do that contributed to Korea's problems in the decade after its liberation? And to what extent did the policies of the outside players involved in Korean affairs after Japan's defeat help or exacerbate the situation in post-liberation Korea?

Arguably the most logical reason to use the "crystal ball" metaphor for that generation of would-be Korean leaders is their familiarity with the endemic problems associated with rampant factionalism in Korean political culture. Koreans who lived through the Japanese colonial era were well aware that excessive factionalism among Korean leaders in the decades before Japan took over had led to backward socioeconomic conditions for most of Korean society, even as elite cliques fared reasonably well materially but proved unable to reach a consensus about a viable international policy capable of coping with emerging trends. As much as Koreans blamed what happened to them under the Japanese upon the Japanese, Korean elites also knew that their own inability to develop an effective alternative to Japan's takeover was a major causal factor. As much as those Koreans felt they had been victimized by the Japanese, they also knew that the Korean nation had been victimized by its own inherent weaknesses—weaknesses within its political culture that facilitated a lack of cohesive leadership and entrepreneurial political initiatives.

That situation was compounded before and during World War II by the ways individuals and groups within Korea aligned themselves either with a Korean stake in Japanese-run activities or with various approaches to oppose Japanese colonialism. This added more layers of factionalism within Korean society, which further complicated the postwar prospects. The Koreans who found themselves liberated from Japan spanned quite a spectrum. Many had suffered under the Japanese. Others had prospered. Many had opposed the Japanese—some very actively, others more passively, and still others only nominally. Among those who supported the Japanese, the same spectrum—active, passive, and nominal—existed. All of these activities produced an array of legacies for survivors to carry into the postwar era, ranging from abject collaborators to heroic figures—including those who "survived" only by the memories of valiant acts they bequeathed to the living through the liberation process. Against this backdrop it is not surprising that Korean society after mid-August 1945 was riven by major divisions linked to prior activities, organized around cliques affiliated with subgroups defined by those activities, and compounded by the society's predisposition toward regional, linguistic, clan-based, religious, and myriad other traditional forms of factionalism.

This made the "in due course" commitment extraordinarily difficult to fulfill in a rapid fashion because the numerous potential leaders of an independent Korean state permitted their clashing interests to prevent them from reaching anything close to a consensus on a common course of action. Part of the problem arose because of the postwar lack of a domestic Korean political base—a taboo idea under the Japanese—upon which returning Koreans could help build a viable independent government. This is not to suggest that Koreans who had remained in Korea as part of the underground resistance were uninterested or apolitical, but they were profoundly inexperienced in genuine politics. This made them ripe for manipulation by Koreans with some political credentials based on their foreign experiences. The domestic groups tried to organize themselves into political parties: conservatives and socialist-communist. The latter included the Korean Communist Party, led by Park Hon-yong, who eventually played an important role in the early years of a separate North Korean government. The Korean Communist Party evolved into the long-standing Korean Workers Party. In contrast, the evolution of political organizations in noncommunist South Korea remained replete with factional maneuvering and frequent relabeling. While the people involved in these early parties could make a claim that they, having persisted under the Japanese mantle, were well positioned to provide leadership for Korea, they were troubled by their lack of serious experience, inability to work together harmoniously, and the fact that many of them were virtually unknown to the American and Soviet victors over Japan who arrived in Korea to oversee the transition to the "in due course" goal.

In contrast, there were two other groups of aspiring Korean leaders with greater credentials from the perspectives of the wartime allies that were about to try to put Korea on the path to sovereign independence. These Koreans were affiliated with the Koreans' supposed shadow government in self-imposed exile which called itself the Korean Provisional Government. Initially based in Shanghai, China, the shadow government, had relocated to Chungking in southern China during World War II. The leading political figures from that organization were Kim Ku and Kim Kyu-shik, both of whom returned from China in November 1945. The provisional organization's main U.S.-based representative and long-term activist was Syngman Rhee, who had lived in the United States for more than thirty years and earned a Ph.D. from Princeton University. Given this background, Rhee had obvious advantages in terms of being familiar with the American way of life, U.S. foreign policy criteria, and the English language. The other prominent political figures whose experiences had centered in Korea or China were not only burdened by the endemic problems associated with rampant factionalism among—and within—the groups they were involved in, most were also disadvantaged linguistically in terms of making their case to the newly arrived Americans and Russians.

This situation was made more difficult for most would-be Korean leaders by post-liberation circumstances that were beyond their control, namely the reasons behind the decisions made by the United States and the Soviet Union regarding how to administratively deal with the Korean peninsula after Japan surrendered. Although President Roosevelt had proposed a tentative arrangement at the February 1945 Yalta Conference for a U.S.-USSR-China trusteeship to guide Korea toward independence, it never materialized. Moreover, as it became evident that the U.S.-led allies in the Pacific theater probably would prevail over Japan, the pressures Washington had been putting on Moscow to have the Soviet Union join the Pacific War finally paid off, when, in the wake of the August 6, 1945, nuclear attack on Hiroshima, the Soviet Union formally entered that theater's war in its last week and sent Soviet troops into northern Korea on August 9, 1945. Since Japan surrendered on August 15, the dispatch of Soviet forces to Korea where—had the war dragged on longer than it did—they would have fought Japanese forces on Korean soil for the duration of the war, the Soviet Union (and its North Korean protégés) could make a case for being Korea's most visible external liberator. These events helped to set the stage for decisions that would adversely influence Korea's future. For U.S. leaders the focus clearly was on dealing with Japan's defeat and preparing to cope with its aftermath in Japan and its imperial outposts, as well as devising the best means bureaucratically to accomplish both tasks. As much as the United States wanted a country with the power of the Soviet Union to join in the battle against Japan in case the war persisted in Japanese outposts despite the major setbacks inflicted by U.S. forces, American leaders understood that the Soviet Union had long-term ambitions vis-à-vis Northeast Asia with roots dating back to Czarist Russia. Because of those concerns, the United States did not want Soviet involvement in the prospective U.S. occupation of defeated Japan. However, given the uncertainties about how Japanese forces in China, Manchuria, and Korea would react to their government in Tokyo's surrender, and given the combination of a lack of well-defined U.S. national interests regarding Korea and U.S. expectations that the "in due course" timetable would be fulfilled rapidly, there was far less U.S. concern about the USSR playing a role in the postwar occupation of liberated Korea.

Knowing that the Russians had considerable familiarity with the circumstances in the Korean nation on their easternmost border and had used substantial numbers of Koreans in the Soviet Red Army, it made sense to U.S. policy makers to have the administrative duties of a brief Korean occupation shared by U.S. and Soviet forces. In part this was a pragmatic judgment call regarding the efficiency of making a transition to an independent Korean state that would presumably have good neighborly relations with both China and the Soviet Union. Since China was not as well positioned as the Soviet Union militarily, nor was Britain, which also was supposed to become involved in a vaguer form of trusteeship per the 1943 Cairo talks, it seemed to make sense to use Soviet assets to facilitate a postwar transition in the occupation of Korea. As much as a logical case can be made for the United States perceiving the Soviet Union in that light, an equally strong critical case can be made that American decision-makers simply did not care enough about Korea to craft a more balanced policy, designed to assure that the "in due course" mandate would be fulfilled promptly and productively. From this perspective, the U.S. geopolitical interest in assuring a Japan-focused set of postwar priorities would be better served by letting the Soviet Union have a proportional share of the action in Korea. This would preoccupy USSR policy toward Northeast Asia so as it could not become a thorn in the side of the United States' plans for occupying Japan. In short, if throwing a de facto Korean geopolitical bone on the Soviet Union's table would distract it for a year or two from interfering in U.S. postwar goals, that appeared to be a satisfactory way to make use of the postwar adjustment process in Korea.

American officials meeting in Washington on August 10, 1945, including a youngish Colonel Dean Rusk, who later in his career became secretary of state, decided that a useful dividing line between the U.S. and Soviet administrative occupation zones would be the 38th parallel across the midsection of the peninsula, thereby leaving Korea's central city, Seoul, within the U.S. zone. This arrangement was suggested to the Soviet side shortly after the USSR entered both the Pacific War and the Korean peninsula. The Soviets accepted that dividing line, even though their attempt to obtain a corresponding northern Japan occupation zone on the island of Hokkaido was rejected by Washington. Inadvertently, this decision to divide Korea echoed an attempt back in 1903 by the Japanese to cut a deal with Czarist Russia that would create zones of influence for the two empires in a divided Korea. The United States' plans to focus on the occupation in Japan and use Korea as a distraction to appease the Soviets, sent ambiguous signals to Koreans, who saw themselves as poised to create an independent Korea. On the other hand, Koreans were largely preoccupied with seizing the opportunity presented by Japan's defeat and seemed content to be able to deal with two occupation powers that claimed to be advocates of a new international world order predicated on decolonization. This struck many Koreans as preferable to the notion of a multilateral international trusteeship, partially guided by Sinocentric Chinese and the British Empire, a notion that seemed more likely to delay Korean independence.

Had tensions that spawned the Cold War not emerged in postwar Europe and spread across Eurasia, a plausible case can be made that the evolution of events in Korea would have yielded an independent Korean nation-state fairly quickly. However, even before Korea's liberation from Japan, the nascent signs of those European tensions were evident. This was reflected early in postwar Korea by the relative degree of enthusiasm and sophistication displayed by the Soviet Union toward occupying Korea—an approach that was similar to the Soviet occupation of much of Central and Eastern Europe. Having entered northern Korea the week before Japan's surrender, Soviet forces had extended their control throughout the northern zone by the time of Japan's surrender on August 15, 1945. U.S. occupation forces did not begin to arrive in southern Korea until mid-September. The head of the U.S. occupation proceeded to organize what was labeled the U.S. Army Military Government in Korea (USAMGIK). More important than that delay, U.S. policy makers did not have a carefully crafted blueprint for what they intended to do in Korea. High-level U.S. expertise regarding Korea was minimal at best, and stood in sharp contrast to the Soviet Union's vision for what it anticipated doing in Korea, which was developed before the war's end. This comparison of the two countries' relative levels of interest in and commitment to Korea versus a number of European countries indicates the reasons why postwar Korea was far less a part of the origins of the Cold War than it was a recipient of an expansive Cold War geopolitical paradigm. For Korea to have been part of the origins of the Cold War, there would have to have been roughly co-equal levels of U.S. and Soviet conflicting interests in Korea, as there were in Europe, and that was not the reality on the ground on the peninsula.

In this setting the aspirants to the creation of an independent Korean nation-state endeavored to generate momentum for their various policy agendas by arguing their case with each other and attempting to persuade the U.S. and Soviet occupiers about the merits of these cases. Given the totalitarian style of the Soviet Union, it was no surprise that their occupation in the northern zone also was totalitarian and predisposed toward supporting both Marxist activists in Seoul and Koreans who had served in the Soviet armed forces. Clearly these were people that Moscow could rely upon to pursue policies that would make an independent Korea amenable to Soviet policies in the region. Similarly it should not have surprised anyone that the United States would be supportive of a free and open society. The trouble was that such a concept was far removed from what most of the postwar Korean political aspirants had experienced. Most of them were far more accustomed to an authoritarian brand of political dynamic, made worse by their predisposition toward rampant factionalism tinged with corruption. As American occupation authorities tried to grasp who these people were and what they represented in terms of Korean political potentials, U.S. policy in Korea did not prove effective.

This whole situation was not helped by the fact that Americans assigned to Korea adapted the guidelines devised for the U.S. occupation in Japan for this former colony of Japan, using some of the institutions and personnel of the former Japanese regime as temporary transition devices. The logic in doing this was based on American recognition that there would be an inadequate number of Japanese-language-proficient American occupation officials to manage affairs on a local level in Japan, hence they would have to draw upon Japanese deemed trustworthy, particularly those with some English-language proficiency, to facilitate communications. Some of this administrative model was applied to Korea, as a territory which was formerly part of an extended Japan. Understandably, the model backfired in terms of Korean readiness to tolerate such a U.S. approach. Virtually all Koreans who were on the receiving end of this policy considered it culturally insensitive and bureaucratically inept. That flawed approach was abandoned, helping to accelerate the return of Japanese to Japan. As a fallback position, the U.S. occupation officials, most of whom had little or no background in Korean affairs—much less any capability in spoken Korean—decided to apply an adaptation of the same bureaucratic model as in Japan, relying primarily upon those Koreans who had served under the Japanese colonial regime but also had some competency in English. This made it possible for the U.S. occupation in Korea to do more or less the same kind of things as the U.S. occupation in Japan was doing, with the important caveat that the occupation period would be of much shorter duration in Korea as the "in due course" commitment was fulfilled.

That bureaucratic mind-set also predisposed American occupation officials virtually from day one toward a degree of empathy toward Korean political activists who had firsthand experience in the United States and knowledge of U.S.-style political standards.[3] Supporters of Syngman Rhee rapidly emerged as the foremost examples of such activists and ultimately he proved to be the primary beneficiary. However, this evolved at the expense of a number of seemingly more prominent political players. Discounted from the outset were several people who received backing from Soviet occupation officials in the northern zone. In the long run the most prominent of these was Kim Il-sung, residing in the Soviet zone, who eventually became the dictatorial head of North Korea. For U.S. purposes the most troublesome of the Marxist group in Seoul was Pak Hon-yong, an activist resident in Seoul who eventually migrated north. He and other leftists joined one of the initial efforts among Korean political aspirants to launch a bid to establish a government that they called the Korean People's Republic. The leader of that group was Yo Un-hyung, better known to Americans at the time by his preferred romanization of his name: Lyuh Woon-hyung. This effort was based on a desire to create a diverse political entity, drawing on leftists, moderates, and some conservatives. Part of its problem was that the definitions of those categories were murky at the time and all of them were riven by factionalism. When coupled with the Soviet endorsement in the northern zone of a hard-core Marxist approach to Korea's independence, American officials in the southern occupation zone rapidly began to treat this group as unduly accommodating to the Soviet-focused activists in the northern zone. While a case can be made that this group's efforts to reach out to the northern zone was primarily motivated by a desire to prevent a rupture between activists in both zones through the establishment of a constructive dialogue process that—if sanctioned by the American occupation leaders—might have enabled the group's more moderate-to-conservative elements to co-opt the other side through persuasion and incentives, that possibility was derailed due to U.S. suspicions about the proclivities of the People's Republic.

The other major effort to launch the basis for a government of an independent Korean nation-state was the Korean Provisional Government. Most of its several hundred proponents had roots in, or ties to, the organization of the same name initially based in Shanghai, that as noted above, had to relocate to Chungking in southern China during World War II along with the shift of the Nationalist Chinese government. This group, which presented itself as the government-to-be in Korea, also drew upon a sizable contingent of

Koreans who had not lived in self-imposed exile in China or the United States, but had remained in Japanese-controlled Korea. Partly because of these people's serious credentials and more or less moderate stature, this swiftly became the group favored by the American occupation authorities. Nonetheless, it too was subject to endemic factionalism, which led it to be emblematic of a society perceived by the Americans on the scene as verging on political anarchy. In short, there was little hope that most of these Koreans could get their political act together in a meaningful and timely fashion. All this tended to legitimize the decision of the United States, made in conjunction with Syngman Rhee's Korea-based supporters, to arrange for Rhee's much-publicized return to Korea on October 20, 1945, from the United States. Rhee had long represented the Provisional Government's case while it was in exile and then pressed for rapid independence after the group's organization of a representative branch in Korea. The best hope for rapid independence among American authorities in Korea was to draw upon Rhee—who was elevated shortly after his return to Korea at seventy years old to be speaker of an appointed interim legislative body that reported to U.S. military authorities—and a cohort that clustered around him. This group was joined by a number of people with significant bureaucratic and corporate experience under the Japanese who also knew enough English to send a signal to U.S. occupation officials that they had some interest in the American approach to politics, economics, and international affairs. The fact that many of these people were familiar with English because they were Christians with contacts to American missionaries also helped to establish a sociocultural rapport between them and the U.S. occupation authorities. Despite the growth of the U.S. occupation's mandate, the United States remained committed to relying on a cluster of Korean intermediaries who were deemed reliable.

Although Rhee eventually came to symbolize the notion of a South Korean client in a Republic of Korea–United States client-mentor relationship, his reputation while in the United States had often been as a difficult person to deal with because of his strong commitment to Korean self-determination—a goal that the U.S. government for decades prior to World War II considered far from central to U.S. policy toward Asia. Even if Rhee's mature, assertive demeanor and the authoritarian faction that rallied to his cause raised concerns among some American observers, he nonetheless presented a viable alternative when juxtaposed to the complex of other factions and would-be leaders—that is, Kim Ku and Kim Kyu-shik, who were better known in China than in the United States. Also an advantage for Rhee was the American sensitivity toward the Soviet occupation forces in the northern zone, which seemed to have been making considerable progress in assembling what was increasingly perceived as a budding puppet regime akin to those the Soviet Union was creating in regions of Europe where it had ousted Naziism.

Partly as a result of U.S. and Soviet political machinations in their respective Korean occupation zones in the initial months that led to the creation of rival systems in the south and north—the former via a muddling through process and the latter via a coordinated agenda—both sides felt a need to try to consult with each other to provide at least the appearance of genuine cooperation. Moreover, since the Cold War was still in a nascent stage, it was always possible that bilateral consultations might yield meaningful results as part of a broader process of cooperation. This was attempted in the form of a United States-USSR Joint Commission intended to develop the means to guide Koreans living in the two zones toward the creation of an independent state. It was launched in December of 1945, met in early 1946, after which it ceased to function for a while, until it was revived in May of 1947. Also during this time span, the U.S. and Soviet authorities in each zone were busy assembling the framework for their respective versions of a desired Korean result. This commission did not accomplish much in terms of its stated goal, but because of its call for a broader dialogue with potential leaders and their organized supporters, fledgling would-be political parties proliferated. Over four hundred parties put in their bid to be heard, most of them lacking much substance. Because of the chaotic undertone of Korea's emerging parties, the rampant factionalism, and the questionable reputation of some potential leaders (Kim Ku, for example, had a notorious reputation for violence), a result of all this was to convince the U.S. and Soviet occupation leaders that each was backing the best available pool of contenders.

This is not to suggest that either the United States or the Soviet Union presented a model that was particularly meritorious. The Soviets were bent on creating a Marxist-Leninist clone that could appeal to Koreans throughout the peninsula with its strong-leader image, and would be aided by the advantages the northern zone enjoyed due to possessing the industrial infrastructure created in the Japanese era as well as the presumed benefits stemming from backing by the Soviet Union with its legacy of a long-standing set of Russian interests in Korea. Conversely, American officials were doing their best to generate a foundation for Korean autonomy so that the creation of an independent state would permit the United States to do what was in the best interests of the United States, namely, hand over sovereign authority to a Korean government, which would help establish a degree of normalcy in the region. This would enable the United States to end its military occupation and pay more attention to more important international issues. U.S. efforts along these lines were impeded by evolving circumstances, which included a stagnant economy in the south, damaged by the loss of a Japanese consumer market and a lack of regular access to the northern industrial base; a surge of Korean refugees (from northern Korea and Manchuria) and returnees (from Japan); and great uncertainty about leadership in the private sector—exacerbated by the lack of an effective Korean governing structure. All of this was made still worse by a sense of social and moral ennui resulting from years of Japanese degradation of Korean values and Korean societal resistance, which tended to legitimize petty crime and corruption, condone disrespect for authority, and accept cutting corners to avoid the letter of the law. Such Korean behavior during the Japanese era contributed to Japanese condescension toward Koreans, which was conveyed to Americans as they took over in Korea and via the U.S. occupation in Japan, in a manner that led many Americans to have low expectations regarding Koreans, which were often fulfilled by these forms of behavior. This level of societal discord and growing poverty amidst a U.S.-backed emerging system that was supposed to value freedom and opportunity, perversely helped strengthen the case being made by the more authoritarian and disciplined emerging system in the northern zone.

The situation in both parts of Korea, but especially in the southern zone under U.S. control, left much to be desired. American guidance for an emerging regime was intended to foster something comparable to what the U.S. occupation in Japan was trying to cultivate in terms of an appreciation for democratic self-determination. However, unlike the Japanese situation where Americans were dealing with a defeated nation prepared to accept guidance and a nation that had experienced a significant degree of democracy in the first quarter of the twentieth century, the Americans dealing with Koreans had to cope with people infused with nationalistic enthusiasm about their independence but who essentially lacked any prior experience with democracy. So, in Korea, this form of political system had to be invented—not reinvigorated. Making this worse, especially among Korean social conservatives, who tended to be seen by American officials as the most stable and potentially productive segment of Korean society, there was a strong tendency to identify the Korean nation in racial and ethnic terms that did not blend very well with the civic values of the systemic paradigm being urged by U.S. officials. Despite these negative factors, in retrospect it is evident that much of what the United States was fostering in the southern zone became the foundation for the subsequent creation of the Republic of Korea. The ROK's roots clearly extend into the ingredients of a fledgling political and military system being created under U.S. auspices. These roots help to legitimize critical analyses that contend fostering this system was the United States' intention virtually from the outset. The problem with this line of reasoning is that the United States almost never displayed sufficient interest in the Korean outcome to justify such a judgment call. The United States may have been a bit naive or utopian in its internationalist expectations about generating broader support for the creation of an independent Korean nation-state via an electoral process encompassing both parts of occupied Korea, but it did pursue that approach—albeit partly as a way to enable the United States to disengage from a geopolitical predicament. The United States' engagement in postwar Korea promised few rewards and posed uncomfortable geopolitical risks, which were exemplified by the warnings emanating from the United States' most conservative and anticommunist cohorts in southern Korea—including Rhee, who pressed the United States to do more to help the southerners prepare a strong self-defense capability to cope with the far-stronger cadre of people with Soviet military experience who were part of the emerging system in the northern zone. There was little U.S. enthusiasm about responding to such southern pressures, which could lead to the creation in Korea of conditions akin to what was developing along the Cold War dividing line in Europe. That lack of enthusiasm was underscored by American concerns that Rhee might well make a move militarily against the northern zone to unify the two areas, if he were provided with the strategic means. American officials wanted to use the still-young United Nations to devise an alternative approach to resolve the emerging gap and tensions on the Korean peninsula.

After trying to guide the southern zone under U.S. auspices with decidedly mixed results throughout late 1945, 1946, and 1947, even as Americans observed the communization of the northern zone under Soviet auspices during those years, Washington launched an effort on September 17, 1947 at the United Nations to create the means to hold pan-Korean elections. This seemed to be a viable alternative given the United States' considerable influence within the United Nations at that time in its history. It established a United Nations Temporary Commission on Korea (UNTCOK) tasked with organizing and holding elections in both zones. Although there were frictions between UNTCOK representatives and the U.S. and Soviet officials after they arrived in early 1948, and unease regarding the relatively chaotic political environment in the southern zone and rigid atmosphere in the northern zone that caused UNTCOK to express doubts about the viability of national elections, they moved forward anyway under pressure at the United Nations from the United States and its supporters. Partly because leaders of the Soviet-guided northern zone argued that the whole process was skewed by U.S. influence to favor a U.S. agenda based in the south with a larger share of the Korean nation's population, but mainly because these leaders had to know they would come up short in any such election, they criticized the process for being unfair, and the Soviet-backed northern zone abstained from the election.

Nonetheless, the United Nations–backed elections were held May 10, 1948, throughout southern Korea. This produced a 198-member National Assembly, with 100 additional seats kept in reserve in case the electoral process could be carried out in the northern zone. This assembly met for the first time on May 31 and announced the name of the country was *Taehan Mingook*, which literally translates as the *big or great Korean people's country*, but is universally known via a looser translation as the Republic of Korea. The assembly also proceeded to draft the ROK's first constitution, which was put into effect on July 17. Under its provisions the National Assembly elected the ROK's first president, Syngman Rhee. This was not a surprise because Rhee's supporters were in the majority in the National Assembly. Rhee, in turn, symbolically announced the Republic of Korea's presence to the world on August 15, 1948, the third anniversary of Korea's liberation. The United States took the lead, joined by about fifty other countries, in granting diplomatic recognition to the ROK. This was reinforced in December of 1945 when the United Nations, in the wake of a UN-sanctioned electoral process, declared the ROK to be the legitimate government of Korea. This did not mean the ROK was a member of the United Nations, a development that would not occur until the Cold War ended.

The trouble was that in the northern zone of Korea none of these developments in the south were accepted as remotely legitimate. On the contrary, they were denounced as the result of a flawed process manipulated by the United States through the United Nations in a Cold War context. More importantly, in terms of the concept of Korea as a divided nation, the UN-sanctioned process was disparaged as a way to carve up Korea and prevent it from becoming a single independent nation-state that could pursue its own policy agenda with its closest neighbors—the Soviet Union and China—as it saw fit. In the context of these denunciations, and in reaction to what the Soviet-backed northerners deemed to be the creation of an illicit regime in the south, the northerners proceeded to go through the motions of an electoral process that allowed them to proclaim on September 9, 1948, the formation of the *Chosun Minjujuui Inmin Kongwhagook*, the Democratic People's Republic of Korea. The processes that they used were murky at best, which was predictable given their Soviet tutelage. This also was reflected in the internal factional maneuverings that had occurred in the northern zone of Korea, which were a blend of the Korean political culture's predisposition toward factional intrigue and Soviet-backed Marxist authoritarianism. This combination of factionalism and authoritarianism yielded a far more obscure and secretive political paradigm, especially when juxtaposed to the relatively open circumstances in the southern zone where Korean squabbles with each other and with their American would-be mentors could hardly be concealed. These maneuverings inside North Korea in the formative stage shall be examined more closely in the later chapter on North Korea's evolution.

For present purposes and to close this chapter on Korea's liberation and division, it is important to note that these two elections, one real—albeit under stress—and the other far less plausible, amounted to a major turning point in the modern history of Korea. After more than twelve centuries of some category of being one territorial state—even if it was not always under Korean control—the Korean nation found itself firmly divided. The Republic of Korea and the Democratic People's Republic of Korea (DPRK) were launched in a Cold War context destined to take each down separate paths. As bad as this was, if Koreans throughout the peninsula had known then where these paths would lead in terms of warfare and more than half a century of hostility, there is little doubt they would have done far more to prevent these paths from emerging and done their utmost to forge the means to remain one nation in one state.

CHAPTER 5

South Korea's Evolution, 1948–2004

Despite the stamp of approval bestowed upon the Republic of Korea by the UN-sponsored elections that spawned the South Korean state, the ROK's early years were decidedly shaky. While the Korean War period, June 25, 1950, to July 27, 1953, was for obvious reasons an intensely shaky phase, the transition from the ROK's founding to the outbreak of war also was unstable. The reasons for this instability center on the concurrent efforts to create a post–Korean liberation independent state, juxtaposed with the emergence of the global Cold War that rapidly enveloped the Korean peninsula. Against this backdrop, this chapter shall address the evolution of the South Korean state from several angles: its geopolitical setting, its political and economic dynamics, and its foreign and defense policies. All of these factors strongly influenced the nature of South Korea's unification policy, which—while noted contextually in this chapter—shall be examined separately in greater detail in chapter 8. The same format shall be applied to North Korea's evolution in the next chapter.

GEOPOLITICAL CONTEXT

Because of the decisions made by the U.S. and Soviet liberators who oversaw its territorial division, the emergence of a South Korean state on the lower half of the Korean peninsula created a geopolitical circumstance Koreans had never experienced in their long history. Many might assume this to be the stark reality of a divided nation-state. There is partial justification for that assumption because Korea's postwar division was a new experience in the history of a united Korean nation-state. However, as described above, Korea had a lengthy experience with multifaceted governance prior to the unified Shilla state and its successors—albeit not a dualistic experience. No, what was a new phenomenon for Korea was the creation in South Korea of a Korean state that lacked direct access to continental Asia because of the total barrier posed by North Korea, making South Korea the functional equivalent of a Korean island-state. This aspect of South Korea's geopolitical situation was dramatically underscored by the ROK's institutional connections with the United States as its strategic and economic benefactor. South Korea's dependence upon U.S. military support, need for U.S. material reinforcement, and awareness that it had to conform to American political and governmental guidance illustrated the ways that South Korea found itself entangled in the U.S.-led camp of the global Cold War. This created another facet of the geopolitical identity of the de facto South Korean island-state, namely, its integration within the United States' worldwide system. This yielded for the first time in Korean history a Korean state that is committed to a major power that is not in Korea's region of the world.

South Korea's adaptation to these circumstances evolved in significant ways from the creation of the ROK in 1948 to the first decade of the twenty-first century. A relatively consistent factor within that entire period has been South Korean anxiety about the reliability of the United States as a distant ally. In South Korea's early (that is, pre–Korean War) years, leaders in Seoul had ample reason to be concerned about U.S. geopolitical consistency because of the lack of a clear U.S. focus on Korea within its post–World War II policy in the Asia-Pacific region. The eruption of war in Korea after North Korea attacked the ROK on June 25, 1950, fundamentally changed that situation. The history of the Korean War, its impact on both the ROK and the DPRK, and its role within superpower relations in the Cold War has been the subject of numerous scholarly studies.[1] This volume addresses that conflict from various perspectives pertaining to each Korea within the contexts of political evolution, international policy, and unification policy. In its geopolitical setting, what is most important about the impact of the three years of the Korean War on Korea is that it simultaneously underscored the division of the Korean nation and greatly intensified the United States' grasp of the issues at stake in Korea.

Thanks to the 1953 United States-ROK Mutual Security Treaty, created after the Korean War armistice on July 27, 1953, which established an open-ended adversarial relationship between the two Koreas and their international backers, Seoul had institutionalized reasons to expect the United States to be a consistently reliable ally. Nonetheless, due to various events within U.S. foreign policy toward Asia—notably, repercussions from the Vietnam War and the normalization of diplomatic relations between the United States and the Peoples Republic of China as well as periodic bilateral U.S.-ROK frictions over economic and political issues that shall be examined in subsequent sections—South Koreans had recurrent reasons for concern about the consistency of U.S. geopolitical logic regarding Korea.

Another source of concern revolved around South Korea's ability to cope with its de facto island status. Despite the commercial virtues of becoming a maritime-oriented state within the free world capitalist camp of the Cold War, the ways that South Korea adapted to that role economically and strategically under the United States' geopolitical wing generated a tendency to be lumped together with an authentic island-state, Japan, which was the United States' predominant ally in Northeast Asia. While that proved to be a major geopolitical asset for South Korea in terms of denoting the ROK's regional importance and creating numerous opportunities, it also proved to be somewhat awkward in terms of fostering "island-to-island" ties between unequal partners with a strained historical legacy. Over time, as South Korea matured politically, economically, and internationally—thereby making the ROK's de facto island status more commensurate to Japan's genuine archipelago status—the ROK-Japan geopolitical relationship and stature from the perspective of U.S. officials clearly grew to be closer to a peer level. This trend became evident in the late–Cold War 1980s and increasingly obvious in the post–Cold War years. As positive as that was for South Korea's geopolitical standing with the wider world, it proved to be an irritant in inter-Korean relations due to North Korea's failure to attain that level of stature within its geopolitical realm. In turn, that geopolitical juxtaposition added to the long-standing problems South Korea faced as a de facto island hoping to merge with the rest of the peninsula that had not experienced this island paradigm. These problems had functional and psychological dimensions based on each Korea's different experiences. Equally important, the prospect of merging a de facto island with a truncated semi-peninsula exacerbated the acknowledged difficulties likely to arise during and after reunification. The more South Korea succeeded as a separate entity, the more all these problems undermined the unification facet of its geopolitical interests.

POLITICAL-ECONOMIC EVOLUTION

South Korean political and economic affairs were profoundly influenced by two aspects of its geopolitical circumstances: the rivalry between the two Korean states fostered by the Cold War milieu and the impact of the United States upon its South Korean ally's domestic affairs. These factors put the Republic of Korea in the anticommunist camp of the Cold War, with manifest political and economic consequences, placing South Korea on a path toward U.S.-style democracy and capitalism. As important as those factors were in guiding South Korea's political and economic evolution, it is crucial to bear in mind that the ROK never abandoned its national roots in either category of its societal evolution. Even though South Korea's experiences since the Republic of Korea's founding in 1948 differed radically from North Korea's experiences, the results in the South drew on the legacy of the entire Korean nation in terms of fashioning a Koreanized brand of democracy and capitalism despite U.S. efforts to act as an influential mentor.[2]

As described in chapters 2, 3, and 4, Korean society throughout its long history was notable for the ways feudal factions and cliques influenced decision-making and shaped the normative values that guided Koreans as they coped with various challenges. These attributes were evident in the political intrigues within the Korean government in exile in China and among its representatives in the United States. When Syngman Rhee became the United States' sanctioned leader in Seoul and de facto founding-father figure for the fledgling Republic of Korea, he brought with him all the heavy-handed factional leadership skills he had cultivated during years of political infighting. Knowing that he would have to cope with clusters of cliques tied to extended family clans, alumni groups, and policy-oriented inner circles, Rhee used what amounted to a strongman leadership model to cultivate loyalty to him. He was helped in this regard by being able to call upon a small group of Koreans and Americans with whom he had interacted while living in the United States. Although this, and the fact that his wife Francesca was a Westerner (born in Austria), facilitated Rhee's efforts to present himself to his fellow Koreans as a leader fully capable of handling the Americans, who were chaperoning South Korea's transition to an independent state, Rhee actually had poor relations with many of the American representatives in Seoul. They, like many U.S. officials who had dealt with Rhee while he was in Washington, found him difficult to deal with on an interpersonal basis. All of this is ironic in the sense that the U.S.-South Korean relationship that began under Rhee and carried on well after he left office was widely perceived as a mentor-client state affiliation. While an accurate overall characterization, President Rhee certainly lacked a clientlike docile demeanor.

Rhee had a volatile personality, demanded personal loyalty, exerted a very tight rein on his followers, and tended to be ruthless with all who opposed him. Had the Korean War not occurred, it is likely that Rhee's leadership style might have damaged the budding U.S.-ROK ties. However, the war reinforced Rhee's use of the strongman model in domestic political affairs. The way the war was fought perversely helped Rhee politically. North Korea's aggression to try to take advantage of an ill-prepared South Korean defense system vindicated Rhee's prewar warnings. The significance of North Korea's attack to the United States' emerging Cold War interests, caused the Truman administration to respond by rallying a United Nations–based coalition of forces, which also bolstered Rhee's standing. The American reaction to having to deal with both the Soviet Union and the People's Republic of China as backers of the North Korean cause also reinforced Rhee's message about South Korea's importance. Even though Rhee's aspirations to prevail over North Korea in the war were not met because the war became a static battlefield struggle which yielded an armistice agreement that left North Korea in place, the war atmosphere certainly reinforced Rhee's stature as South Korea's acknowledged leader. Rhee also underscored his hard-core anticommunist credentials by his prewar and wartime stridency in opposing North Korea's vision of unifying Korea by force of arms. This created a legacy of anticommunist resolve and support for strong ROK defenses among subsequent South Korean leaders, which strongly influenced Korean politics until well into the post–Cold War era.

The political party Rhee created and dominated, the Liberal Party, was decidedly conservative in its domestic and foreign policy orientation. It was prone to demonizing its opposition in a McCarthyite manner for being leftist and unpatriotic. Although the party's use of the "liberal" label may seem contradictory, it actually was not, in that classical Western liberal political philosophy can connote values often found in today's conservatism worldwide. Their pragmatic reason for using the liberal political label for the ruling party was because it fit well with the liberal U.S. Democratic Party running the U.S. government when Rhee assumed office. In that regard it is important to note that the main opposition party during Rhee's years in office was called the Korean Democratic Party, even though it was as socially conservative as Rhee's ruling party. South Korea's real leftists were largely eradicated as a political force. Such political views did not resurface in South Korea in a credible manner until late in the twentieth century. More important than these interparty nuances was the reality that neither party was well developed as a political organization with genuine grass roots. Both adhered to the strongman model, and tended to be authoritarian, hierarchical, and dominated by cliques prone to corruption. These parties thereby created a precedent for weak political party structures, building on Korea's Confucian tradition in their focus on personal and clan loyalties, which inhibited South Korea's democratic evolution.

This situation was not helped by the economic backwardness that engulfed South Korea during Rhee's rule. Coming out of the Japanese colonial era, wherein Korea's material advances were offset by Korean frustrations over being mistreated, post–World War II Korea clearly fit a third world paradigm. South Korea's relative lack of an industrial base, compared to North Korea, added to these problems. In turn, the damage to the infrastructure caused by the Korean War massively compounded the initial bleak prospects for the South Korean economy. However, the intensified commitment of the United States to South Korea spawned by the Korean War's place in the Cold War, combined with the emotional bond created by wartime casualties, enabled South Korea to benefit from major U.S. and UN economic aid programs. Had the Rhee government been more adept, the post–Korean War period of the 1950s could have launched a major turning point for the South Korean economy. However, the Rhee regime was ill prepared politically to make such a move and was not very innovative bureaucratically. Nor did it heed domestic economic reformers prepared to revive a Japanese-derived model adapted to South Korea's needs. The Rhee regime merely acquiesced to the limited goals of U.S. aid donors to simply keep South Korea's economy from collapsing. The net result was a stagnating South Korean economy made worse by Rhee's political machinations and consequent corruption throughout the 1950s.

After having been elected by the National Assembly in 1948, Rhee used Korean War era martial law to change the presidential selection process in 1952 to a popular vote system. He was reelected that year. While a step forward in terms of mass democracy, Rhee's move was motivated by his inability to control the opposition forces and confidence that mass voting could more easily be manipulated. That confidence was put into operation during the 1952 and 1956 elections, which Rhee maneuvered to victories. To run in 1956, Rhee pushed a constitutional amendment through the National Assembly, allowing him to run for more than two terms. Then in 1960, at age eighty-five, Rhee ran again and won in a March 15 contest that was widely perceived as rigged. That victory caused a student rebellion on April 19 during which over one hundred people were killed in the course of controlling it, leading to expanded unrest. In part because ROK Army officers, who also saw the need for basic reforms, publicly backed the students' cause, conditions in Seoul became sufficiently unstable that the United States intervened diplomatically and persuaded Rhee to step down from the presidency and go into exile in Hawaii on April 26, 1960.

South Korea was poorly positioned to cope with this upheaval. Although the United States facilitated this transition and encouraged South Korean democratic advocates to pursue a genuine form of democracy, U.S. leaders were not very active in supporting the evolving processes. An interim government supported by the United States moved rapidly to create an improved constitution, put in place July 15, 1960, using a parliamentary system with a prime minister and president selected by the National Assembly. This system became known as the "Second Republic" after it failed and was replaced nine months later by the "Third Republic." It did not fail because of systemic flaws. Arguably it could have moved South Korea toward full-fledged democracy. However, once again Korean factionalism, cronyism, and corruption got in the way. The dominant party, the Democratic Party, evolved from what was formerly Syngman Rhee's main opposition. As its members maneuvered to back various candidates, the result was overly freewheeling maneuvering and discord. Although the resulting prime minister, Chang Myon, and the largely figurehead president, Yun Po-sun, had solid backgrounds, they were unable to foster a stable governing system because of the excess factionalism that undermined its operations. In essence those who pursued democracy in the Second Republic pushed for too much, too soon. They could not meet their goals because the roots of the old South Korean political culture inhibited progress and South Korea's struggling economy complicated the prospects for political reform. Had the military not enjoyed the level of power in South Korean society that it did at that juncture, the Second Republic might have muddled through. On balance, the best that can be said about the failure of this attempt to build a democracy in South Korea,[3] is that it simultaneously set the stage for the mixed record of success and failure that characterized the subsequent regimes and thereby whetted the appetite of well-informed South Koreans for what might have been, if the Second Republic leaders had been more skilled politically and had been helped more attentively by the American benefactors in Washington.

South Korea's political and economic destiny was transformed by a military coup, May 16, 1961, led by ROK Army Major General Park Chung Hee. The Park regime lasted until his assassination, October 26, 1979. During those years, it earned a mixed reputation as a very authoritarian regime verging on a dictatorship at times, but a regime that achieved major successes on the economic front. The eruption of a military coup in South Korea came as a shock to U.S. officials working on Korean issues because they assumed the ROK military, which had been created and had grown significantly under American tutelage, had absorbed American civil-military values that would forbid the military from waging a coup. While ROK forces had grown to over 600,000 personnel by mid-1953 and during the rest of the 1950s had become a very sophisticated military organization, learning from its U.S. counterparts, its leaders were a mixed lot—younger officers who adhered to the role model exported by the United States and older officers whose military roots were largely drawn from the Japanese era. Park Chung Hee was in the latter category and the architect of the coup, Lieutenant Colonel Kim Jong-pil, was from the former. He also was Park's nephew via marriage. While many of the more senior officers were as faction-ridden and amenable to profiting from bureaucratic cronyism as their civilian politician counterparts, Park's readiness to lead the younger generation's aspirations for a better-regulated national system gained their trust, plus his affinity for the prewar Japanese martial values put him in a position to command a coup designed to shake up a troubled system.

Initially the military junta, operating as the Supreme Council for National Reconstruction, blocked civilian political activity and installed Park as the ROK's acting president. Ostensibly their motives were to purge South Korea of its tendency toward corruption and revive its brand of Confucian moral values, which had been weakened in the colonial era and sidetracked under American guidance. The Park junta was being pressured by the United States in its early stages to make a quick transition to a stable civilian-led system. By August of 1961, Park announced the supreme council would turn over power to civilian authorities by 1963. The junta emitted purposefully ambiguous signals about its intentions. Although Park and his cohort were actually creating the foundation behind the scenes for what would become South Korea's new ruling party, the Democratic Republican Party (DRP), in public they pretended to be on a U.S.-favored track. In part this level of uncertainty, exemplified by Park's promise in February 1963 not to run for president, was caused by doubts generated by scandals erupting in the Korea Central Intelligence Agency (KCIA), launched a month after the coup under Kim Jong-pil's direction. These scandals forced Kim to step down, but he then became even more of a behind-the-scenes power broker. Park ran in the October 1963 elections, winning a relatively narrow victory over the Second Republic's figurehead president, Yun Po-sun. However, because the opposition candidates for the National Assembly were fragmented by factionalism and their experiences under the junta, Park's DRP won a clear majority in the assembly. This enabled Park and company to move on from the initial ambiguous phase in his rule to a far more structured approach to political and economic developments.

In what amounted to the second phase of Park's rule, from late 1963–1972, he concurrently emphasized strengthening his party base while launching a very structured economic reform package which reinforced the political goal of reducing ambiguity. In contrast to Syngman Rhee's animosity toward Japan, Park appreciated what Japan had accomplished and—as part of his diplomatic efforts to establish ROK-Japan diplomatic ties—he adapted the Japanese developmental paradigm for Korean purposes. On the economic front, he used a five-year-plan format that went on until after his assassination. Its use of guided capitalism, with a strong state role that originally focused on breaking out of the stagnant mold inherited from the earlier republics, was aimed at agricultural modernization and industrial self-sufficiency. This focus shifted over time to more of an emphasis on balanced economic interdependence and claims to being a free trade advocate. In reality, the Park administration's use of an adapted Japanese model reflected a corporate state old boy network drawing on Confucian values that was quite protectionist. Just as the Japanese situation was labeled "Japan, Inc.," Korea's became "Korea, Inc." with big business and big government interacting closely. Throughout the 1960s and 1970s, South Korea incrementally shed its stagnant economic qualities and was rapidly playing catch-up in cooperation with its two main economic partners: the United States and Japan. That economic agenda was reinforced by the spillover benefits South Korea experienced from the Vietnam War, in which ROK forces supported the U.S.-South Vietnam cause and Korean firms at home and in Vietnam profited.

Politically, Park was more discreet about adopting a Japanese model. Nonetheless, the methods that Japan's ruling party, the Liberal Democratic Party, had used to control societal factional frictions were adapted to Park's more authoritarian regime in order to create a de facto social contract between the masses and the political and economic elite. This system worked well, enabling Park to boost his legitimacy and to help him prevail in two more elections, 1967 and 1971, putting the legacy of his coup further in the past. His opponent in the April 1971 election, Kim Dae-jung, accused Park of rigging the victory. Kim then began an effort to fight back, aided by domestic unrest in the summer and fall in response to a combination of an economic slump and opposition to Park's authoritarian style. These developments, plus the regional setbacks being experienced by the ROK's alliance partner, the United States, in the Vietnam War, which led the United States to withdraw one of its two infantry divisions assigned to Korea in 1970, provoked Park to declare a national emergency in December 1971. The declaration was made to respond to internal stresses and to the possibility that North Korea might perceive these as an opportunity serving its interests.

Even though these circumstances had calmed down by early 1972, Park persisted with his authoritarian reforms in the form of a series of emergency measures and the imposition of martial law in October. This set the stage for a November 1972 referendum under duress that authorized Park's *Yushin* (Revitalization) Constitution, which greatly strengthened the president's direct power and weakened the National Assembly by giving the president power to appoint a third of the assembly members. It is important to note that the word *Yushin* is the Korean pronunciation of the Chinese ideograph used by Japan's leaders in the 1868 Meiji *ishin* (restoration) that marked Japan's serious modernization efforts. Given Park's other usage of Japanese examples for Korean purposes, this choice of words is significant. The Yushin-based system became South Korea's "Fourth Republic." Although this system was intended to make the "Korea, Inc." economic-political approach more effective by building on grass-roots campaigns such as the New Village (*Sae maul*) movement, designed to broaden the benefits of societal change, and it did enjoy economic successes, its dictatorial qualities aggravated internal tensions and worsened Park's human rights image, especially with the United States during the Carter administration.

A major consequence of this was to stir up popular support for opposition politicians. Kim Dae-jung was the most vocal opponent at home and abroad, leading to his kidnapping in August 1973 by the KCIA while touring Japan. The United States had to intervene to save his life. He and other progressive politicians, notably Kim Young-sam, rallied the opposition forces and set the stage for their future presidencies. Park's dictatorial reputation worsened the political climate in South Korea and encouraged opposition to him overseas. One of his opponents from Japan attempted to assassinate Park in August 1974, but missed him and killed Park's wife. After that episode Park became increasingly cautious about interacting with the public, underscoring his aloof authoritarian style of politics. Amidst this partisan turmoil, Park's regime in its last years experienced labor unrest, intellectual ferment, and frictions among the military, which saw its former institutional clout being eroded by corporate powers. All these factors contributed to the bureaucratic tensions that led a prominent official, KCIA Director Kim Jae-kyu, who felt offended by how he had been treated by members of the presidential staff, to assassinate President Park on October 26, 1979, on the Blue House grounds—Seoul's version of the White House.

Park's assassination unleashed a political process that was reminiscent of the post–Rhee period in the ways free democratic expressions yielded a return to authoritarianism. The popular mood in the wake of Park's assassination blended remorse with relief. Guided by Prime Minister Choi Kyu-hah, as acting president, potential successors quickly tried to expand their support base. The most prominent were the "three Kims"—conservative Kim Jong-pil using the Democratic Republican Party that increasingly had become a facade in Park's latter years, and two progressives, Kim Dae-jung and Kim Young-sam using their New Democratic Party. As these contenders scrambled to line up factions, an intramilitary coup occurred on December 12, 1979, designed to purge the old-school cronies among the Park-era military elite and replace them with younger officers whose professional credentials were deemed superior. The leader of this coup was Major General Chun Du-hwan, who was in charge of investigating Park's assassination, and a key supporter was Major General Roh Tae-woo, both of whom became successors to Park as president.

As support for the three Kims' campaign grew to a fervor in early 1980, Chun exerted pressure to limit the ardor in ways that provoked large-scale violent antigovernment demonstrations on many university campuses in Seoul on May 15, 1980. These were repressed under martial law imposed by Chun via the acting president's authority. This unrest spread rapidly to a new center in Kwangju on May 17, unleashing what amounted to an open rebellion in a part of the Cholla province that had once been in the forefront of an insurrection against Japanese colonial authoritarianism. The de facto revolt was crushed by the ROK military with an official acknowledgment of two hundred casualties and nonofficial estimates in the two thousand range. That controversial military action was made still more controversial because of suspicions that the ROK military would not have been able to redeploy sizable forces to cope with the political unrest without some level of U.S. awareness, and perhaps approval, of the reassignments of South Korean forces operating within a U.S.-led military command structure. In the wake of these events, at Chun's direction, acting president Choi on May 31 installed a Supreme Committee for National Security Measures. Because of Chun's intramilitary coup and the ways Chun manipulated the security system after that internal event to create the Special Committee—with its distinct echoes of Park's supreme council, noted above—Chun's assumption of power has been widely perceived as a political coup comparable to Park's. Despite the nuanced differences, Chun's takeover and his subsequent succession by Roh Tae-woo perpetuated the political paradigm of South Korea's government being run by a military-backed clique.

The Chun government, known as the "Fifth Republic," 1981–1987, was a military-linked regime. For a couple of months, Chun's Special Committee played strong-arm politics with dissenters, arresting and trying those it viewed as extremists. By August 16 acting president Choi resigned, clearing the way for Chun, who had promoted himself to the rank of four-star general in the interval, to be selected as temporary president via a remnant electoral college of Park's Yushin system on August 27, 1980. Following an in-house constitutional revision that created a seven-year presidential term in office, Chun was elected again on February 25, 1981. All of this reinforced the parallels between Park and Chun. However, unlike Park's regime, Chun inherited a socioeconomic system that was far more sophisticated and prosperous. While this was a major asset, it also compelled Chun and company to be more attentive to the legality of their regime and pay more attention from the outset to the political appearance the regime conveyed.

Chun's means for this task was the transformation of Park's Democratic Republican Party into Chun's new ruling party, the Democratic Justice Party. Although this party was an instrument for a cliquish hierarchy to manage factional tensions, it also emphasized creating grass-roots networks throughout urban and rural areas. While the motive behind this party transformation was to solidify support for Chun, it also was useful in terms of easing the human rights pressures South Korea experienced during the Carter administration and facilitating smooth political relations between the Chun and Reagan administrations. Chun's efforts to build an institutional base for his party was most important in terms of the ways it symbolized a shift away from the Park-era political paradigm. However, it also created a precedent that later led to more party building. This tendency was reinforced throughout the Chun years by his administration's need to cope with the changing nature of the "Korea, Inc." model as the business and labor wings of society became more interdependent with the electoral support for the civilian bureaucratic wing, thereby diminishing the direct clout of the military wing. Furthermore, all of these factors became more politically sensitive to South Korea's increasing consciousness of its global geo-economic interdependence and need to present a positive image. In turn, this was complicated by domestic political frictions over major power (especially the United States and Japan) economic pressures to follow their open market advice, which yielded growing support for protectionism. Chun was able to use these circumstances to bolster his political support. The more the ROK economy prospered, the more South Korean ruling party political dynamics evolved away from overt authoritarianism and toward more subtle forms.

Amidst this political diversity, Chun was trying to set the stage for Roh Tae-woo to be his successor and create a role for Chun as a behind-the-scenes power broker. That plan fell apart as a byproduct of the student-led popular protests in 1987 that were exacerbated by heavy-handed crackdowns and as a result of the media atmosphere created by Chun's successful efforts to arrange for the Summer Olympics to be held in Seoul during 1988. This opened the door to closer international scrutiny and severely constrained Chun's ability to manipulate the political processes in South Korea. Chun's most radical opponents seized this opportunity to wage major prodemocracy demonstrations, which led to clashes with police who cracked down on them. It rapidly became obvious that Chun's plans were slipping into disarray. This necessitated a rapid change in how to pass the leadership role on to Roh. Although Roh shared the same military legacy with Chun, he and his advisors fashioned a new image for Roh as an "ordinary person" (*potong saram*), who could personally relate to the aspirations of his fellow citizens, in order to enhance his electability. In late June 1987, Roh proposed constitutional reforms with direct presidential elections and amnesty for Kim Dae-jung, permitting him to reenter the political process. Roh's constitution was approved in a national referendum in October 1987.

This political atmosphere also opened the door for the three Kims to refocus their efforts by creating political parties with authentic grass-roots networks to support their various causes. These were Kim Jong-pil's alternative conservatives in the New Democratic Republican Party, and progressives—who having created Kim Youngsam's New Korea Democratic Party in 1985—relabeled it the Reunification Democratic Party in mid-1987. After Kim Dae-jung's political rights were restored, he and his followers split the progressive movement by starting the Party for Peace and Democracy. Although all these parties subsequently changed names as conditions evolved, and illustrated a tendency toward autocratic personality-oriented parties, they also represented progress in democratic pluralism in South Korea. As positive as this pluralism was, and despite the fact that it yielded a more genuine form of democracy, in the short run it was intended as a divide-and-conquer way to take advantage of factional tendencies among political rivals. In the December 1987 elections, the votes were divided, permitting Roh to prevail without a majority and to make a case that South Korean democracy was functioning. His approach to reform politics helped to calm the country and permitted his administration from 1988–1992 to incrementally guide the ROK toward more open politics that also aided its economic progress because of the improved international image it could convey. Roh's agenda included bureaucratic reforms, greater reliance on the National Assembly, where party diversity also increased, and a readiness to crack down on corruption—including in the Chun era.

The three Kims sought to benefit from these political changes by adapting to the new environment during 1988–1989. By the end of 1989, Roh and the three Kims attempted to create a new consensus. Kim Dae-jung's more progressive posture prevented him from going along fully. This yielded a coalition between President Roh and the other two Kims, conservative Kim Jong-pil and liberal Kim Young-sam. They joined together to form a new big-tent party—the Democratic Liberal Party (DLP) that had many parallels with Japan's long-standing ruling party, the Liberal Democratic Party (LDP). Liberal critics lambasted Kim Young-sam for selling out, but in reality he used his position in the new party to change the dynamics of South Korean politics by co-opting a spectrum of conservatives into his brand of moderate liberalism. Using his gradually increasing influence in the DLP, Kim Young-sam positioned himself to become the heir apparent for Roh's tempered style of conservatism. Kim Jong-pil's conservatism could not compete adequately. In effect a moderate liberal, Kim Young-sam, co-opted the system that supposedly had co-opted him. As this was occurring from 1990–1992, Kim Dae-jung carved out a political role as the principled dissenter.

In December 1992 using his big-tent approach, Kim Young-sam was elected president to replace Roh Tae-woo, putting South Korea's DLP on a path very similar to Japan's LDP. In reaction to his party's loss, Kim Dae-jung ostensibly quit politics, a decision he reversed as soon as circumstances called him back into the arena. In the background of South Korean politics was the United States' experiences with President Bill Clinton's "new Democrat" model of a moderate politician redefining what had been a more liberal party. President Kim Young-sam's supporters perceived him as Korea's Clinton by virtue of supplanting conservatives within South Korea's ruling party, and Kim Dae-jung reinvented himself as a Clinton-like comeback kid. These external role models became still more obvious after Japan's LDP experienced a major setback in 1993, causing Kim Young-sam and the DLP's leaders to relabel their party the New Korea Party. The other "two Kims" followed suit in early 1995. Kim Jong-pil's conservatives became the United Liberal Democrats and Kim Dae-jung's progressives became the National Congress for New Politics. Despite these additional name changes, and ongoing efforts to strengthen their grass-roots base, South Korea's political parties remained remarkably personality-centered in ways that permitted an autocratic leader to exert control over factional tensions.

Amidst these reshuffles, Kim Young-sam throughout 1995–1996 dealt with corruption and Kwangju-related charges against his predecessors, Chun and Roh. These were resolved in the 1996 trials that sentenced Chun to death and Roh to prison for twenty-two years in August 1996. By the end of the year, Chun's sentence was commuted to life in prison and Roh's term was cut to seventeen years. These events reinforced President Kim's stature as an advocate for clean government. By the end of the following year, both sentences were lifted and they were released. That, coupled with the eruption of various corruption scandals in his party and the bureaucracy, hurt Kim's image and caused his opponents to explore new political options, including experimental cooperation between the other two Kims. Throughout the early portion of Kim Young-sam's time in office, South Korea's economy appeared to be on a stable course of prosperous maturation, marking continuity from the Park, Chun, and Roh years. All that began to get shaky in early 1997, in response to growing economic uncertainty in 1996. A combination of labor unrest against government-backed liberalization designed to make corporate use of labor more flexible, the financial collapse of a major conglomerate (the Hanbo Group), and serious questions about the merits of Korea's banking system raised political questions about the leadership capabilities of the ruling elite. This was exacerbated when President Kim's son was arrested in May 1997 on bribery charges.

The ruling party tried to perpetuate its control via the December 1997 presidential election by backing a former judge with a "Mr. Clean" reputation, Lee Hoi-chang. En route to the elections, the other two Kims, who headed their parties' tickets by the spring, took advantage of the ruling party's problems and splinter parties' activities when in August 1997 they surprised political observers by forming a coalition in support of Kim Dae-jung's candidacy. In practice, this was Kim Jong-pil's version of Kim Young-sam's former cooption maneuver. As all this was evolving, the South Korean economy was being rocked by the Asia-wide 1997 economic crisis, spawned in 1996, which was most acute in Southeast Asia, but in Korea raised serious political questions about how to deal with corruption, banking standards, the prospects for more corporate bankruptcies, and international pressure for market reforms and less protectionism. Hurt by its image as the party in charge during this escalating crisis, the ruling New Korea Party tried to be innovative by merging with one of the splinter parties in November to form what they referred to in English as the Grand National Party, whose Korean name, the *Hannara dang*, means the One Nation Party.

These political maneuvers were overshadowed on the eve of the December 18 presidential elections when the ROK government on December 4 had to call on the International Monetary Fund (IMF) for a $55 billion rescue package that required Korea to accept corporate and bureaucratic reforms that would open it to greater foreign influence. These circumstances hurt the ruling party, leading to Kim Dae-jung's election. Before he took office in February 1998, South Korea's currency lost half its exchange rate value (from 800 won to 1,660 won per U.S. dollar), and the ROK received emergency aid from the IMF. Prior to taking office, Kim Dae-jung waged an effort to build confidence in his economic plans and to spread the focus to a larger political and economic agenda of inter-Korean reconciliation based on his Sunshine Policy. He also designated conservative stalwart Kim Jong-pil as his prime minister—a reward for his coalition campaign support and as means to create liberal-conservative legislative support to cope with socioeconomic problems. As odd as this team was, bearing in mind each one's role in the Park Chung Hee era, it was a striking example of how South Korean democratic processes had matured and helped set the stage for further moves in that direction. Once in office the Kim Dae-jung (he was widely referred to as "DJ") administration moved rapidly to pursue economic, social, and political reforms in keeping with his progressive legacy, which was tempered by a pragmatic need to work with amenable conservatives in his coalition. The early portion of DJ's term in office was dominated by economic issues, supplemented by his desire to press forward on the inter-Korean front with his Sunshine Policy, the details of which shall be addressed in chapter 8.

Although Kim Dae-jung's reputation had been based on a legacy of reform and criticism of corruption, which he was able to build through legal measures focused on the preceding Kim's administration, DJ also was damaged by accusations against the practices of his administration. This atmosphere was intensified by private watchdog groups dedicated to scrutinizing Kim Dae-jung's and his opponents' ways of governing. Toward the end of 1999, hoping to reduce pressure from critics and looking toward the year 2000 and a new century, DJ announced tentative plans to rename his party the New Party for the New Millennium. DJ's fragile coalition with some conservatives fell apart in early 2000 when Kim Jong-pil resigned as prime minister to try to enhance conservative stature through National Assembly elections. Shortly after that, DJ finalized his new party's name as the Millennium Democratic Party (MDP). Yet again this was another example of a Korean political party being centered on the identity of its leader, rather than a well-structured organization. Although DJ's political standing in polls had dropped seriously because of his mixed political and economic record, that slippage and his overall reputation rebounded for a while after he was awarded the Nobel Peace Prize in October 2000 for his Sunshine Policy efforts to engage North Korea in a constructive dialogue.

As the Kim Dae-jung administration struggled to cope with its problems via renewed anticorruption efforts, the September 11, 2001, terrorist attacks on the United States altered the international arena in ways that were felt politically within South Korea. Against the background of President George W. Bush's early 2002 controversial "axis of evil" statement that included North Korea, South Korean politicians who aspired to succeed Kim Dae-jung began to sort themselves out with regard to where they stood on this issue. Amidst more intense criticism of DJ's performance, conservatives debated among themselves to see who could be best positioned to succeed him. By the spring of 2002, looking toward the December presidential election, the progressives nominated a decidedly liberal candidate, Roh Moo-hyun, to lead the MDP. As the campaign evolved, Lee Hoi-chang, making a repeat run on the conservative side, seemed destined to win and was treated by the United States as a virtual president-in-waiting because of the rapport he displayed toward the Bush administration, which appeared to help his prospects within South Korean society. Roh ran a fairly radical campaign, drawing on his background as a human rights lawyer, in which he stressed ROK independence from foreign pressures and promised he would never "grovel" for foreign approval. In doing so Roh played to growing popular resentment over how the United States was dealing with North Korea and with surging anti-Americanism that resulted from U.S. handling of a U.S. armed forces legal incident. Despite earlier expectations, Roh won the election by a narrow margin.

The Roh Moo-hyun administration took office in February 2003, and in its early phase (as of this writing in 2005) has had a very mixed track record. He and most of his appointees have been very liberal, leading his conservative critics to liken them to North Korean ideologues. Partly because of his working class personal background and decidedly progressive political orientation, liberal support groups expected a great deal from him. When he failed to deliver on their terms, Roh's poll ratings plummeted, activist groups began to second-guess him, and he had repeated clashes with the press. By the end of 2003, Roh admitted that he was not doing well as president, left his own party, and speculated about having a popular referendum on his performance. In March 2004 conservatives seized the moment by launching an impeachment drive based on Roh's legally questionable support for a political reform movement, this temporarily removed Roh from office, replacing him administratively with his prime minister. His most radical supporters fought back, reorganizing their movement as a new party, the Uri Party (Our Party), which proceeded to win in National Assembly elections, leading the ROK Constitutional Court to reinstate Roh as president. This led Roh's standing to rebound and gave him a new ruling party with progressive views. As troubled as the Roh government was by uncertainties surrounding his leadership style, by the way his uneven relations with President Bush affected South Korean politics, and by socioeconomic unease on the labor front, this government can legitimately claim to have expanded the democratic process in South Korea beyond any of its predecessors and to have caused a much broader spectrum of activists—supporters and opponents—to become engaged in determining how South Korean political and economic development will evolve. While it is far from certain how this evolution will transpire, this is a very positive development that promises not only to keep South Korea on the path to well-grounded democracy and economic reform, but also promises to greatly reduce the likelihood of any more military coups.

FOREIGN AND DEFENSE POLICIES

Compared to many other countries, with the obvious exception of North Korea, South Korea's foreign and defense policies appear to be afflicted with a split personality.[4] One aspect of these policies copes with the rival Korea while the other aspect copes with the rest of the world from nearby neighbors to far-flung countries. Of course some of the rest of the world—notably the United States, China, Russia, and Japan—has a strong vested interest in how each Korea deals with the other. Reinforcing this split personality metaphor is the bureaucratic reality in each Korea that dealing with the other Korea is logically treated as an intranational task rather than an international issue. Hence it cannot truly be part of foreign policy. Similarly, with regard to the ROK's defense policy, leaders in Seoul certainly know what they are defending and who they are defending against. Nonetheless, they also know that the ROK's defense interests amount to a seminational form of defense in which one half of the Korean nation is defending against the other half at the same time as it has to keep one eye on the security interests of the entire nation as it will eventually be reconfigured after unification. For these reasons the topic of both Koreas' approaches to reunification, which shall be mentioned in passing where necessary here, will be largely left to the two concluding chapters on the two Koreas' efforts to rebuild one Korean nation-state.

In South Korea's early years, prior to the establishment of the ROK in 1948, it could not officially have a foreign policy or a defense policy, since it did not exist as a sovereign state. It existed under the auspices of U.S. occupation forces that had liberated it from Japan. As U.S. officials supervised the installation of the elements of a regime that would evolve into the ROK, there was no doubt about the fledging government's external priorities. From a theoretical perspective, they had to pay attention to what the Soviet Union was doing in northern Korea in case the Soviets either persuaded the Americans about the wisdom of their vision or the U.S. forces simply declared their mission accomplished and departed, leaving the peninsula in Soviet hands. In a similar vein the group of pre-ROK would-be leaders also had to pay some attention to what was going on in China, in case both the U.S. and Soviet forces decided to opt out, letting China resume its traditional Sinocentric hierarchical role in the region. Despite the degree to which U.S. officials had not been well prepared to assume responsibility for sharing Korea's post-liberation future, it quickly became evident to the Koreans under their purview that the United States was in charge for the foreseeable future. Hence for these Koreans who were hoping to become the leaders of an independent Korea by influencing the decisions of the U.S. chaperones, their equivalent of a foreign policy was of necessity virtually totally focused on the United States.

That pattern was reinforced by the United States' role in the creation of the Republic of Korea under the auspices of the United Nations. From the day the ROK was launched, the focus of its foreign policy was to assure its survival, reinforce its international legitimacy by making the case for incorporating the entire peninsula under its mantle, and build support for both of these tasks. From the start it was obvious that one country dominated these agendas: the United States. Throughout the ROK's existence that truism has remained intact. What has changed over time, however, is the degree to which the ROK has emphasized its focus on the United States within its foreign and defense policies. A useful way of visualizing this evolution is to think of the ROK's policies as a sequence of pie charts that show the ratio of foreign influences upon Seoul as well as the volume of South Korea's involvement in international affairs. Very early in the ROK's history, the United States' proportion of the pie chart would be nearly 100 percent. However, the importance of the international affairs substance symbolized by the pie chart was quite small in that early phase. Over time the United States' share of the pie has decreased as other countries became relatively more important to the ROK than they had been. But that decreased U.S. share of the South Korean pie still constituted a growing ROK-United States relationship because of the rapidly growing volume symbolized by the pie. This metaphor helps one visualize how the pattern of ROK dependence upon the United States internationally has changed dramatically as a ratio, but remains very much intact as the foundation of its foreign and defense policies. In other words, the ROK's former client-state relationship with the United States has eroded, but in a very positive manner indicating an economic, political, and military maturation process that reflects well on both South Korea and the United States. That long-term process is reflected in the trends of South Korea's foreign and defense policies during its succession of governments, trends which shall be outlined here.

The Syngman Rhee government policies, coupled with U.S. officials' focus on broader U.S. interests as compared to Korea-focused interests, clearly warranted the client-mentor paradigm. Nonetheless, Rhee was far from a docile client. He and his cohort were very pushy in trying to get the United States more attuned to Rhee's vision of bringing all of Korea under one government. Before the Korean War, President Rhee's pressure had little effect other than to annoy U.S. officials. The Korean War clearly was a turning point for Rhee's policy agenda. It greatly strengthened Rhee's arguments on behalf of a stronger ROK and more U.S. support. The war put a United States-ROK alliance on a firm track, made South Korea's defense priorities versus North Korea clear, and laid the foundation for subsequent ROK quests for economic development aid from the United States and other wartime international supporters under the auspices of the United Nations. On the other hand Rhee was not a supporter of the Korean War's armistice resolution because it stopped far short of the victory he wanted. So, just as Rhee remained a stubborn client, he also became a disgruntled client, who wanted the ROK's American benefactor to be more actively supportive of his vision for the entire peninsula. That vision was stridently anticommunist, which fit well into the United States' growing Cold War role, but it also was markedly out of step with the United States because of Rhee's anti-Japanese attitudes. These attitudes were reflected in South Korea's resistance to U.S. pressure for its two Northeast Asian allies to be more cooperative. Most important within this vision was Rhee's hope that the United States would become more proactive in support of his aspirations for what a later generation of Americans would label "regime change" in Pyongyang. Clearly that did not happen. The remainder of Rhee's time in office throughout the 1950s was focused on getting the United States to cooperate on his not very innovative societal development agenda through economic aid programs and building the ROK defense establishment, so that it would be able to defend against future aggression by North Korea.

Rhee's defense agenda had unintended consequences in terms of creating more than the firepower the ROK wanted in order to cope with the DPRK. It also fostered an expanded military bureaucracy with its network of factions that spawned the Park Chung Hee coup described above. Although the coup formed a temporary setback for ROK-United States relations, in terms of ROK defense policy it had positive consequences by creating circumstances that led to three decades of South Korean governments led by people with military know-how and vested interests in creating a more viable form of ROK defense. The coup and its legacy also sent a signal to North Korea about the kinds of leaders they would be confronting in their southern rival. Even after the military-backed governments in South Korea faded and more democratic purely civilian leaders took office, since the early 1990s South Korea's defense policy remained largely on track in terms of growing technological capabilities and military professionalism.

On the foreign policy front, the post-Rhee decades have been much more subject to the international forces which give rise to the evolving pie chart ratios. The Park Chung Hee administration's foreign policy remained closely tied to the United States after getting past the initial U.S. resistance to how he took control. His largest accomplishments went hand in hand with each other. Park's development of socioeconomic ties with Japan and ROK-Japan diplomatic recognition in 1965 was predicated on his government's readiness to use Japan as a developmental model, despite serious domestic critics. By going down the same economic path as Japan, South Korea moved rapidly toward expanding its international network of commercial partners. In turn, this led to the ROK trying to enhance its image as a legitimate international player and more than a U.S. client. South Korea's moves in that direction were ironically helped by the ways it behaved in a clientlike fashion when responding to U.S. requests for dispatching ROK forces to fight in South Vietnam. Although North Vietnam was not a threat to South Korea, Seoul was a major contributor to the U.S.-led coalition for several reasons. Primarily it was due to a sense of obligation to help in circumstances analogous to how others had helped the ROK in the Korean War. Beyond that, Seoul was anxious about the negative implications of not helping, in terms of retaining a U.S. commitment to South Korea. Also, by militarily helping the United States, when Japan was abstaining, Seoul knew it would bolster U.S.-ROK ties and give its post–Korean War military forces invaluable field experience. South Korea also acquired unexpected benefits by committing to Vietnam in terms of the economic spillover into ROK development patterns and gaining corporate credibility as an overseas contractor in Indochina, which led to an expansion of ROK economic opportunities in many other parts of the world. In short, South Korea's foreign policy significantly matured, thanks to the foreign economic horizons that were expanded via the Vietnam War.

In contrast to those generally positive developments, the Park years also experienced several foreign policy rough spots. Park's dictatorial reputation hurt South Korea by getting it lumped together with other authoritarian states that many analysts scorned as pariah states. Park's efforts in Vietnam and the economic results these efforts spawned helped to mitigate South Korea's image problem, but did not eradicate it. On another mitigation front, Park displayed skill in balancing a hard-line anticommunist stance that worked reasonably well in terms of coping with North Korean efforts to undercut the ROK, with tempered efforts to establish a diplomatic dialogue with the DPRK. However, those efforts did not blend well with Seoul's troubled ability to adapt to an awkward situation, created when the Nixon administration began the U.S.-PRC diplomatic normalization process that persisted through the Carter administration.

The latter period also posed problems for the Park government due to Carter's human rights criticism of the ROK and plans for post–Vietnam War U.S. force cuts in Korea. Those issues caused major problems for Park that escalated due to South Korea's ham-handed efforts to try to buy influence in Washington, which blew up in the form of the infamous Koreagate scandal.[5] In tandem with those issues, the Park government also experienced economic problems as a result of the 1973 OPEC oil crisis, during which South Korea could not get the same degree of U.S. support that other allies, notably Japan, received. That caused the ROK to become far more conscious of and responsive to its various natural resource dependencies and gradually move toward reaching out to countries that were suppliers. Due to this series of problems, juxtaposed with Park's successes, his administration learned yet another lesson from Japan in terms of adapting a low-profile political face to South Korea's role in world affairs. South Korea's commercial successes would encourage a variety of countries to see the ROK as something other than a dictatorial pariah state prone to stumbling. Despite Park's rough spots, his administration succeeded to putting the ROK solidly on that path and providing a foreign policy legacy that all of his successors have built upon.

This was most obvious in the two military-linked governments that followed, under Chun and Roh. During the Chun years, the dichotomy between a hard-line domestic policy and a more innovative foreign policy grew. Building upon Park's outreach efforts to assure greater consciousness of international interdependence, which importantly was in stark contrast to North Korea's emphasis on its *juche* doctrine of self-reliance, the Chun government rapidly expanded South Korean relations in Europe, Latin America, the Middle East, and Africa. Chun also used the momentum generated by the 1986 Asia Games and the 1988 Seoul Olympics to extend various invitations to political and cultural groups to visit Seoul and expand their familiarity with South Korea. Among those invited were representatives from the Soviet Union and the People's Republic of China. The essence of what the Chun administration was doing was to expand upon Park's tentative interdependence model and begin the process of adapting it to Japan's comprehensive security paradigm, which defined national security in more than military terms to include interdependent economic and cultural harmony that would inhibit tensions and conflict. Japan's example in reaching out to a broad spectrum of countries and its use of the 1964 Tokyo Olympics to improve Japan's image were also influential factors behind Seoul's foreign policy innovations under Chun.

The Roh Tae-woo administration built upon Chun's advances by adapting West Germany's *Ostpolitik* model for reaching out to East Germany en route to a dialogue designed to facilitate German unification, in the form of South Korea's *Nordpolitik* system, launched in 1988. Its essence was an effort to simultaneously have both Koreas reach out to the four major powers looming in the background—the United States, the Soviet Union, China, and Japan—so that improved bilateral ties could hasten a multilateral dialogue process. Since North Korea was not very well positioned to follow this model, this diplomatic initiative amounted to a way to do an end run around the DPRK, put the ROK on a fast track to improved relations with all four of the major powers with a stake in Korea, and nudge South Korea's foreign policy toward a form of bilateralism-based multilateralism well in advance of the end of the Cold War, when such multilateralism would become more widespread. In those terms South Korea during the Roh administration was well ahead of the curve in global trends.

Against that background, South Korea from 1989–1991 experienced a series of transformative events which were part of the larger process of ending the Cold War that led Seoul to adapt its foreign and defense policies to the changing times. The fall of the Berlin Wall and German unification, the dissolution of the Soviet Union and reemergence of Russia, and the publicity surrounding U.S. military power in the Persian Gulf War collectively reshaped South Korean foreign policy. Each of these deserves attention because of the way each altered the circumstances in which South Korean foreign policy was made, compelling Seoul to emphasize a reactive approach—rather than a proactive approach to shaping its foreign policy.

Arguably the most complex situational change was how German unification evolved more rapidly than most South Koreans had anticipated it would, causing a profound reappraisal of Germany's value as a model for the two Koreas. The impact on Korean unification shall be assessed in later chapters, but it is important to note the way the precedent created by German successes and its impact on the European geopolitical balance heightened Seoul's consciousness of other countries' interest in the prospects for inter-Korean reconciliation and unification plus the geopolitical consequences for Asian stability. This became a significant factor in South Korea's relations with the United States, Japan, and China because of each one's interest in the possibility that Korea might go down the same negotiations path as Germany. The split personality–facet of ROK foreign and unification policies was blurred as a result of the impact of German unification because of the ways Seoul had to incorporate its approach to inter-Korean relations more overtly within its overall foreign policy.

The end of the Cold War was made more graphic by the collapse of the Soviet Union and the widespread media publicity received by the United States' status as the world's newly preeminent superpower during the Gulf War. This also altered the context for South Korea's foreign policy because of the impact these events had on North Korea. While that impact is covered in the next chapter, it is important to note succinctly that North Korea was both shaken and emboldened. These changes caused many countries to be more concerned about the DPRK than they had been previously, which forced South Korea to pay more attention to those concerns within ROK foreign policy. Even though South Korea was in the winning camp of the Cold War and had an ally that was now universally recognized as the world's strongest country, these developments—as was the case regarding German unification—also compelled Seoul to incorporate its approach to inter-Korean relations within the ROK's overall foreign policy. Seoul had to because other countries assumed that was integral to the ROK's foreign policy.

These factors contributed to the creation of ROK diplomatic ties to Russia and China, ROK entry (along with the DPRK) into the United Nations, far greater attention in Seoul to the means for balancing ROK relations with China and Japan, and mounting uncertainty about how the United States might cope with a post–Cold War peace dividend. These issues are addressed further in chapter 7. The new circumstances also increased Seoul's interest in global and regional multilateral organizations that could give South Korea more platforms for pursuing its foreign policy agendas. In short, the foreign policy pie charts were evolving rapidly.

One interesting aspect of how the ROK's foreign and defense policies were influenced by all these changes pertains to South Korea's acceptance of an out-of-its-region security role through the United Nations. For many South Koreans, the United Nations was primarily known for its role in starting the ROK, being the organization that facilitated the U.S.-led coalition that fought on the ROK's behalf in the Korean War, and for much of the post–Korean War era, the United Nations was the venue for neutral nations observers on the DMZ. That changed after the Cold War and when both Koreas became member states of the United Nations. Beginning in Somalia in 1993, the ROK undertook UN peacekeeping operations (PKO) as a way to demonstrate that it possessed the means and the willpower to behave responsibly on behalf of the international community. South Korea in subsequent years was involved in other PKO missions in the Western Sahara, East Timor, Cyprus, and Georgia. These activities reinforced the ROK's perception of the importance of international interdependence, presented a positive image of South Korea, and illustrated the ways that its confidence in inter-Korean reconciliation processes is sufficient enough to allow Seoul to have security responsibilities in other parts of the world.

South Korea's growing optimism about its foreign policy expectations in the early post–Cold War era was disrupted by three major events which left lasting legacies that are still being dealt with. Two are Korea-focused. North Korea's pursuit of a nuclear option and use of reckless brinkmanship diplomatic tactics has caused myriad problems for South Korea. Starting with the Kim Young-sam and Kim Dae-jung administrations, these problems went well beyond the potential threat of using nuclear weapons. The United States' reactions to the DPRK almost led to war in 1994 and caused several rifts in ROK-U.S. interactions which were inherently damaging, providing a wedge issue for North Korea to weaken the ROK-United States alliance, and generating momentum behind improved ROK-PRC relations, which could eventually have a negative impact on Seoul's ties to Washington. This issue also was complicated by South Korean sensitivities to how the United States during the Park years blocked ROK development of a nuclear option and how the United States seems to use a double standard when dealing with North Korea compared to several other countries—including Japan. The United States' policies toward North Korea's nuclear option caused numerous problems for Seoul because of views that the U.S. ally was not sufficiently attuned to ROK interests, including on the reunification front. That aspect was underscored by ambivalent U.S. reactions to Kim Dae-jung's Sunshine Policy overtures toward North Korea and DJ's prominent June 2000 summit diplomacy with Kim Jong-il that earned him the Nobel Peace Prize.

The other Korea-related event was the 1997–1998 economic crisis assessed above. Given the way South Korea had used its growing economic stature as the foundation for an expansive and innovative approach to many countries around the world, the economic crisis, the fall of the ROK currency's value, and the need for an IMF rescue package severely undermined the international prestige Seoul had relied upon to build a more sophisticated foreign policy. On balance, this crisis shook outsiders' confidence in South Korean economic stability and caused the Kim Dae-jung and Roh Moo-hyun administrations to have to adjust to open market reforms that did not mesh well with their brand of progressivism. Their resulting domestic political problems influenced their ability to be creative on the foreign policy front. Despite the major consequences the economic crisis had for South Korean assumptions about harmonious interdependence, Seoul rebounded and continued to emphasize its version of comprehensive security.

The third major event was not directly related to Korea. The 9/11 terrorist attacks on the United States caused reverberations in all U.S. relationships with its allies—including South Korea. Although Seoul supported the initial U.S. responses to the attacks, over time frictions developed between the George W. Bush administration and both the Kim Dae-jung and Roh Moo-hyun governments. The ROK was not supportive of the unilateralist aspects of the Bush doctrine, Bush's use of the "axis of evil" metaphor, his open loathing of Kim Jong-il, nor of U.S. pressure on the ROK to commit forces where the United States wants them—most notably in Iraq, or the United States' use of post-9/11 armed forces transformation goals to rearrange and redeploy U.S. forces in Korea, without what the South

Korean leaders deem to have been adequate advance consultations. The deployment of ROK forces in Iraq became particularly contentious. Seoul's previous willingness to dispatch ROK forces to help in UN peacekeeping missions did not cause nearly as much controversy in South Korea as Seoul's consideration of the Bush administration's request for ROK forces to join in the Iraq coalition. In short, in the post-9/11 atmosphere South Korea simultaneously has felt empathy for the United States' endangered situation blended with anxiety over how the Bush administration has handled the problem, which has adversely affected ROK relations with the United States.

As significant as these issues are, it is crucial to note in concluding this section, in keeping with the evolving pie chart metaphor explained above, that the United States remains by far the foremost international partner for South Korea. Although no longer a client-state, and led by a current president, Roh Moo-hyun, who emphasizes ROK independence, South Korea still treats the United States as a mentor. The difference is that the ROK has added others to the mentor category, notably both China and Japan. Of the two, given Japan's mixed legacy, China is more likely to be competitive with the United States as what might be called a peer mentor. Thus, in terms of South Korea's future foreign and defense policies—short of it being merged into a unified Korea—one can speculate about how the ROK will balance the United States and China, what circumstances might induce Seoul to tilt decisively toward one or the other, and what the consequences of such a tilt would be for each player and for the region as a whole.

CHAPTER 6

North Korea's Evolution, 1948–2004

The North Korean half of the Korean peninsula is a dramatically different state compared to South Korea. Radically different politics, economics, and values have yielded a Korean state that is the focus of enormous attention throughout the world.[1] Prior to examining how North Korea has evolved since its founding, it is important to note two aspects that shall distinguish this chapter from the preceding chapter on South Korea. First, compared to analyzing the accurate data available on the Republic of Korea, the Democratic People's Republic of Korea's extraordinarily secretive nature makes analyzing it a formidable task necessitating a great deal of reading between the lines. Second, compared to South Korea's political evolution throughout successive governments, North Korea has been dominated by one regime with many layers of nuance. Consequently assessing North Korea requires an approach appropriate to its peculiarities that can draw upon comparisons to the much better factual data available regarding South Korea and the shared heritage of the former Korean nation.

GEOPOLITICAL CONTEXT

In contrast to the uncertainties surrounding South Korea's early years following Korea's division, the founding of two rival states in 1948, up to the Korean War, North Korea had a far less shaky start. Part of the reason for northern Korea's better situation had to do with its physical circumstances. Unlike South Korea, which had to cope with becoming a de facto island cut off from the connecting land that appended the Korean peninsula to the Asian continent, North Koreans dwelled in territory that retained its peninsular characteristics. Of course, from a North Korean vantage point the southern "island" became a serious impediment in terms of how it evolved societally and its strategic ties to a threatening major power from the other side of the Pacific Ocean. Moreover, the southern "island" compelled North Korea to deal with a territorial identity that would have pronounced bicoastal attributes. Nonetheless, even if North Korea was a truncated peninsula, it was still a peninsula—a fact that permitted North Koreans to be very comfortable with their geographic identity and its extensive ties to Korea's historical origins, including its cultural bonds with its largest physical neighbor, China. The territory under North Korea's purview also sustained high levels of confidence because the Japanese colonialists had focused on the northern peninsula for industrial development due to its wealth of natural resources—especially its mineral deposits and hydroelectric potential—as well as the locations of its ports. As a result of that era, many northern Koreans also acquired skills that led to North Korea starting off with a considerable advantage in terms of human capital. The overall situation was reinforced by the innate level of confidence predicated on northern Korean regionalism and provincial subregionalism, which sustains northern biases toward southerners within the Korean nation. Given those stereotypes, which complicate inter-Korean relationships, the fact that their part of the divided nation had such physical and spatial advantages seemed to be a literal natural advantage preordained by some higher power.

As noted in the previous chapter, in sharp contrast to South Korea's initial lack of a mentor with a well-developed interest in Korea or a cogent vision for what it wanted to do in—and for—

Korea, from the day the Soviet Union became involved in its transition, North Korea benefited from a Soviet plan intended to guide Korea toward recovery as a nation-state on the USSR's far eastern border. To North Korea this relationship was a major asset because many northern Koreans, including those who had dwelled in Japanese-controlled Manchuria, had looked at the Soviet Union to their north and northeast as an opponent of what Japan represented to Koreans and as a place where they could escape. Some Koreans migrated to the Soviet Union and while there developed an appreciation for the Soviet system as an alternative to Japan in terms of its societal merits. These Koreans, upon their return to Korean soil were especially appreciative of the Soviet Union's vision for Korea and saw it as superior to the vague notions expounded by the American occupiers of the other half of Korea. In short, North Koreans were extremely confident that their territorial advantages went far beyond the physical merits noted above. They were convinced that Korea's proximity to Soviet territory motivated the Soviet Union to hit the ground running with a well-defined notion of where they were going and why in terms of Soviet and Korean national interests.

In addition to such Koreans, who became central to the political, economic, and military evolution of the DPRK, a spectrum of other Koreans also had relations with the pre-liberation Soviet Union in ways that led them to be favorably disposed toward the USSR's geopolitical vision for Korea. Many of the Koreans who organized themselves as guerrilla fighters against the Japanese oppressors found support from the Soviet Union in their efforts to sabotage Japanese control. Because of the proximity of the Soviet border to northern Korea's industrial base, many of the guerrillas focused on the northern peninsula and Manchuria. This was reinforced by historical memories of Korean volunteer militias in that region, which had played such a major role in fighting against Hideyoshi's invasion in the sixteenth century that these Soviet-backed guerrilla forces saw themselves as doing it again to the hated Japanese. Similarly, those Koreans who found their way out of colonized Korea into China and lent their support to the Soviet-encouraged communist revolutionary forces determined to create a Chinese regime modeled on the Soviet Union, also saw themselves as part of an anti-Japanese cause whose patriotic acts would help liberate Korea.

Given North Koreans' self-perceptions of having been in the heartland of the anti-Japanese guerrilla movement, after Korea's liberation from the Japanese via Japan's defeat by the allied powers, it was not much of a stretch for the North Koreans to believe that Koreans had played a truly significant role in the defeat of Japan. When coupled with North Korea's proximity to both China and the Soviet Union, its cultural bonds with China that included an affinity for China's continentalist strategic mind-set, and its ideological ties to the Soviet Union and China's communists, North Korea in its fledgling stage was predisposed toward accepting the Soviet vision for Korea and the geopolitical parameters that shaped that vision. That perspective was reinforced by South Korea's emerging ties with the United States because of the Soviet view of U.S. policies as imperialist and because the United States' post–World War II policy in Asia became predicated upon a Cold War strategy using Japan as geographical base. This made U.S. policy look as though it was influenced by Japanese regional interests, and given the history of Japan and the United States with regard to cutting deals at Korea's expense, this tended to reinforce North Korea's geopolitical ideology.

Over time the Korean War, ongoing ROK-DPRK tensions, DPRK ties with the communist world's two major powers—both on the DPRK's northern border—plus U.S. leadership of the anticommunist camp in the Cold War pushed North Korea further into a rigid geopolitical position. This had many repercussions for North Korea's domestic developments as well as its role in regional and world affairs. Among the many other countries on the communist side of the Cold War, North Korea was positioned to become one of—if not *the*—most rigidly totalitarian Marxist regime(s), bent on protecting what it perceived as North Korea's mission to defend the interests of the entire Korean nation.

POLITICAL-ECONOMIC EVOLUTION

In many respects North Korean political and economic affairs have been the mirror opposite of what transpired in South Korea. Certainly the two Koreas evolved in opposite directions. Nonetheless, the DPRK was influenced by the same series of factors that did so much to shape the ROK, namely the rivalry between the two Koreas and the impact of the United States upon its South Korean ally. Beyond those factors, however, the DPRK became a radically different state because of an odd combination of socioeconomic models that influenced its evolution. Far more than South Korea, North Korea remained true to what it perceived to be Korea's traditional heritage—albeit a distorted interpretation of that heritage. At the same time, and partly responsible for that distortion, North Korea—like South Korea—looked to its Cold War supporters as a model. Unlike the United States-ROK client-state metaphor, however, DPRK relations with the Soviet Union and the PRC exerted pressures to be ideologically pure, mixed with confusion about precisely how to define that purity, as China and the Soviet Union experienced a rift, compounded by Korean cultural desires to devise a Korean nationalist version of an ideological paradigm.

Undoubtedly the central figure in shaping the political evolution of the DPRK was the person who warrants the honorific title of founding father, namely, Kim Il-sung. He was and is, years after his death, universally known as the "Great Leader" (*Widae-han Chidoja*); virtually divine qualities are ascribed to his leadership, and the aura surrounding him is revered. He was born in 1912 and lived until 1994, when his death jolted North Korea to such an extent that it has never fully recovered. His life, writings, but most of all his actions collectively shaped the DPRK in ways that are utterly different from anything that transpired in the ROK. In light of the way North Korea eventually evolved, it is important to acknowledge that the path it followed was not preordained by either the initial circumstances in North Korean society or by a Soviet blueprint of any sort.

When Soviet forces entered Korea to help liberate it from the defeated Japanese, the human raw material for a communist regime was relatively limited. There were Marxist intellectuals in Korea, but relatively few in number. They helped to reestablish a small Korean Communist Party based in what had been Korea's capital under the Japanese, Seoul, which remained the administrative capital of the postwar American zone. The original Korean Communist Party had existed during the colonial era, but its excessive factionalism and Japanese repression led to its failure to be effective. The revived party's leader was Pak Hon-yong. Despite the significant number of workers in northern Korea's industrial base, under the Japanese they had never been allowed to cultivate any significant labor consciousness. Just as was the case in imperial Japan proper, the Japanese rulers in Korea had been pointedly anti-Marxist. Faced with these conditions, the Soviets attempted to implement their communist vision for post-liberation Korea by getting Koreans with significant experience in the Soviet Union or with helping the Chinese communists with revolutionary activities to return home to build a viable Stalinist-style system for Korea. Sensing the opportunities being presented to them, various Koreans on site throughout the north tried to formulate their views and postures to conform with what the Soviets were advocating for Korea. As a result of this admixture of disparate elements, and Koreans being Koreans in drawing upon their political culture, there was a tendency toward factional alignments that were often not based on principles the Soviet mentors thought appropriate.

Despite the Soviet vision for Korea, which contrasted to the relative lack of such a vision on the part of U.S. occupiers further to the south, early on in the north, the process was not jelling because of factionalism and poor credentials on the part of many aspirants to power. Just as Americans eventually reached out to English-speaking Koreans, including several who had lived in the United States, the Soviet leaders drew upon Russian-speaking Koreans with experience in the Soviet bureaucracy or armed forces to help focus the tasks at hand. Among them, but by no means selected by the Russians to be the future "Great Leader," was Kim Il-sung. Kim had credentials in terms of his father's role in anti-Japanese activities in Korea, which caused his family to go into exile in Manchuria. Kim, whose birth name was Kim Song-ju, did something that occurs periodically in East Asian societies, namely, adopting a martial pen name or what the French call a nom de guerre: Kim Il-sung. There also is a version of this name change that ascribes the assumed name to an earlier anti-Japanese guerrilla fighter whose name, Kim Il-sung, was adopted either as a legitimately honorific gesture or, opportunistically, in order to bask in his aura as a surrogate. Which version is accurate is a source of controversy among some Korea scholars. On balance, what really matters is that the person the world knows as Kim Il-sung was engaged in the anti-Japanese armed struggle with Soviet support and was considered by Soviet military leaders to be one of their own.

Exactly how much support Kim Il-sung really had among Soviet officials also is debated. It is relatively clear that Kim enjoyed such support, but it is clear that others had Soviet support too. What Kim also had was enough political skill to use other would-be leaders either for his own purposes to get them aligned behind him, based on Korean factional tendencies, or for their own purposes by encouraging them to engage in interfactional squabbles, which amounted to a divide-and-conquer political strategy. He was helped in this strategy by being a relatively new face in the competition, with an aura of success against the Japanese, unlike some of his competition whose flaws were more evident. Through this combination of political maneuvers, reinforced by his ability to draw on Soviet support, Kim Il-sung generated momentum toward building a personality-oriented hierarchical system of factional loyalties with himself at the apex. Kim and his supporters, as well as some rivals, made use of the Soviet vision for postwar Korea by establishing a North Korean branch of the Seoul-based Communist Party. Because of being in the Soviet-run zone, this branch became more effective and dynamic than what was nominally the party's center. When northern and southern Korea slipped into a divisive pattern as their two external mentors' relationships hardened amidst an intensifying Cold War, the northern branch of the Korean Communist Party was transformed into the North Korean Workers Party (NKWP) in 1946.

While these events seen in retrospect clearly set the stage for what was to develop in North Korea, prior to the formal creation of the ROK and the DPRK in 1948, it remained plausible that political moves within the northern zone of Korea could have moved toward one post-liberation Korean nation-state. The factional maneuvering among northerners was similar to that occurring among southerners and both groups might well have merged had Cold War pressures not intensified. The major political difference between the two Koreas at that juncture was the focus of the Soviet vision versus the vagueness of a U.S. vision. Against that backdrop northern political activists could see what approach would benefit their quest for power and understood what type of Marxist, one with Soviet credentials, warranted support. In contrast, the options suggested to the southerners were more diverse. Consequently the northerners were being guided toward a form of hierarchical authoritarianism capable of building on Korea's Confucian traditions to channel factionalism in a Stalinist style. This infused the northern political machinations with a sense of purpose that the more freewheeling southern political scene had difficulty achieving, despite Syngman Rhee's strongman model.

The situation in both Koreas was made more acute by the U.S.-led moves to use the United Nations to hold Korea-wide elections. As explained in chapter 4, this yielded the creation of the ROK and the DPRK, in that succession. Northerners and their Soviet mentors saw no reason to participate in a procedure that would be to their disadvantage in terms of potential voters. Moreover, they had reason to hope that whatever emerged on the other side would prove to be unstable and lack sufficient U.S. support to remain viable. Accordingly in the course of rejecting the UN electoral process as valid for all of Korea, North Korean political activists became increasingly entrenched in an authoritarian Stalinist model. Although Kim Il-sung also had roots in that Stalinist system, during the DPRK's formative stage, several former Soviet bureaucrats who were familiar with the Communist Party of the Soviet Union played prominent roles in transforming the NKWP into the Korean Workers Party (KWP), intending to make it the communist party of all of Korea, including in the ROK where the remnants of the southern branch were falling apart. In an odd way all these maneuvers helped to serve Kim Il-sung's political interests by enabling him to be proactive in criticizing many of those other politically active leaders for being overly bureaucratic in their demeanor with the result that the systems they were fostering would be too stilted to serve the purposes of the DPRK's development. This was odd because the means Kim Il-sung used to rally supporters around his cause relied on his Stalinist-Leninist branch of Marxism, which used the legacy of the Soviet system and the results this yielded amounted to a highly structured cult centered on Kim's persona. In short, by organizing his followers in a very disciplined fashion, drawing on Korean political culture's tradition of controlling factional tendencies, Kim also produced for the DPRK a bureaucratic dictatorship.

The main vehicle for this state system was the KWP, with Kim firmly at the controls. In sharp contrast to South Korea, where political parties experienced a sporadic evolution and did not develop solid grass-roots support until well into the ROK's democratic maturation, Kim's communist party swiftly became rigidly hierarchical, tightly disciplined, and conscious of the need for its version of grass-roots in the form of mass membership. Unlike its Soviet or Chinese communist mentors, the KWP evolved into a party with many more rank-and-file members. But this should not be seen as representing the voice of the people to the elites of North Korean society. Its purpose actually was to give the elites, with Kim Il-sung at the absolute center of the political, economic, and strategic decision-making universe, the eyes and ears necessary to keep tabs on potential challengers, detect factional cliques that could be disruptive, and thereby serve as the means for conducting a series of purges.

The societal evolution of North Korea, as was true of South Korea also, experienced its first major turning point during the Korean War. The foreign policy ramifications for North Korea of that watershed shall be examined below, but in terms of the DPRK's politics, economics, and security policy, the war was a traumatic event causing major changes on all fronts. The war was the result of North Korea's aspirations to bring all of Korea under the DPRK's purview by unifying Korea and extending Kim Il-sung's political vision of a Soviet-style state adapted to Korean culture. Kim and his cohort perceived this as being in the best interests of the entire nation. Had they succeeded militarily, that aspiration would have been fulfilled. In retrospect it is clear that Kim Il-sung and those in the Soviet Union who encouraged the DPRK's bold aggression had misunderstood U.S. policy in that stage of the Cold War and underestimated American resolve. As the DPRK experienced serious reversals by the end of 1950, the stage was set for a far more protracted conflict than Kim Il-sung had anticipated, which unleashed profound North Korean reappraisals of what had gone wrong and how to rectify it. In turn, this led to a series of purges designed to weed out individuals who could be blamed for poor judgment or incompetence. On the face of it such efforts could be seen as logical steps, but because these measures were laden with ideological overtones, they effectively put

North Korea on the track to an almost puritanical form of Stalinist-style fanaticism. However, because what evolved from this political process bore the indelible stamp of Kim Il-sung's mantra of a North Koreanized brand of Marxism, Korean politics rapidly became infused with what became known as "Kim Il-sung thought," a state philosophy based on his and his core advisors' efforts to answer what had gone wrong as a result of the Korean War. Reinforcing the tight political control over the North Korean people legitimized by the strains of the Korean War was the economic and infrastructure damage inflicted by U.S. bombing attacks on the DPRK. The advantages possessed by North Korea as compared to South Korea were largely wiped out as a consequence of a war that North Korea had brought upon itself. In that context, tighter political control helped to mitigate the chances of popular unrest in reaction to these material losses.

Further compounding North Korea's problems, and in contrast to the diverse wartime assistance South Korea received from countries that then became useful in their postwar reconstruction assistance, the DPRK did not receive as much strategic assistance from a spectrum of countries. Its initial Soviet mentor did not help nearly as much as its PRC benefactor, which contributed sizable forces to a shared cause with the DPRK. In addition to the consequences of PRC aid for North Korea's foreign policy parameters, the fact that China intervened for national defense reasons that were very different from the internationalist rationales behind South Korea's benefactors created the famed "lips and teeth" relationship with China that exerted major political pressures within North Korea. The Kim Il-sung authoritarian adaptation of Stalinist examples came under pressure to adapt to a Maoist paradigm. Given Korea's past experiences with learning from Chinese political culture, this pressure had profound implications. Furthermore, since both the Soviet Union and the PRC were preoccupied with their post–World War II and post–revolutionary war efforts to develop their own economies, neither was in a good position to help North Korea recover from the material damage done by the war.

Traumatized by the failure to achieve its goals in the Korean War, the DPRK in the postwar era reacted to its setbacks by reorganizing its political and military administrative hierarchy with successive rounds of purges that solidified Kim Il-sung's dictatorial regime. Kim also attempted to rebuild North Korea's shattered industrial base and revive its economy using a series of tightly structured state-designed and -implemented plans. However, the rigid state system the regime was solidifying proved to be inept at such practical affairs over the longer term, even though for the short term, during the postwar 1950s, the DPRK rebounded enough to appear to be ahead of its southern rival. That yielded the unintended consequence of motivating the ROK's emerging leaders to catch up to and surpass the DPRK even as North Korea was engaged in policies that would lead it toward serious slippage.

Making matters worse for the rigidly authoritarian and increasingly secretive North Korean regime, which, unlike its South Korean counterpart, could not draw upon vibrant U.S. and Japanese models, the DPRK explored a series of flawed Soviet and PRC models. Drawing on China's efforts to do more for itself when Soviet aid was not sufficient, North Korea experimented with greater self-reliance, labeled a *juche* doctrine in 1957. While this mass movement did not achieve much, the Kim regime has persisted in using the concept in revised forms over the years. Almost half a century later, it still remains a factor in North Korean socioeconomic rhetoric, albeit in a significantly altered format. Two other mass movements were notable at the turn of the 1950s. One was the DPRK's rapid mass production scheme called the *Chollima undong* (the flying-horse movement), derived from the Soviet Union's Stakhanovite movement and the PRC's Great Leap Forward movement. The other was the *Chongsang-ri* movement (named after the site where it was launched), modeled on China's *Hsia Fang* (downward) movement, that was intended to get state bureaucrats to interact with workers in a manner that would foster an appreciation for working-level problems. North Korea's efforts failed as much as its two external models did.

At the same time as these failures were evolving during the late 1950s and early 1960s, the PRC and the Soviet Union were experiencing difficult times as their respective brands of communism proved to be less than compatible. This yielded the famous Sino-Soviet split that led to a gradual shift in the Cold War dynamic. Its consequences for DPRK foreign policy shall be addressed below, but it also had major consequences for North Korea's domestic evolution. North Korean advocates of Soviet and PRC models, which were proved inadequate, when coupled with the DPRK's inability to gain much from a troubled broader communist camp in the Cold War, discredited such advocates and further strengthened the already formidable hand of Kim Il-sung. His approach to the *juche* concept evolved toward an adaptation of autarky predicated on North Korea's need to shape its own—and the entire Korean nation's own—future without being dependent upon external powers. While this is often perceived as Kim's abandoning the core principles of Marxism, and there is an element of that at work, it also amounted to Kim embracing a more nationalistic Korean interpretation of Marxism with touches of Leninist ideas about group discipline that would work well for controlling Korean factionalism. Just as various communist parties in Europe explored what became known as Eurocommunism when the opportunity presented itself later in the Cold War, the DPRK under Kim Il-sung's tutelage amidst the Sino-Soviet split developed a Kimist school of Marxism in order to meet DPRK needs in ways that the paradigms exemplified by Stalinism, Maoism, and a sequence of Soviet successors to Stalin could not do.

The result of all this was the creation of what has been aptly described as the Kim dynasty. Although that term assumed a different, and more literal, nuance by the 1970s when the process of institutionalizing the DPRK line of succession within Kim's family gradually became evident, well before that stage Kim Il-sung's embrace of a fusion of nationalized Marxism with Korea's traditional notions of hierarchicalism yielded a North Korea that displayed links to Korea's past dynasties. As much as the Kim regime disavowed such ties and its advocates scorned the notion of a so-called Kim dynasty, Kim Il-sung and his immediate cohort acted in a manner reminiscent of Korean monarchs and their courts replete with tiers of royalty. One result of this was in very sharp contrast to the political evolution that occurred in South Korea from the 1950s to date. In the DPRK, one leadership line, one party, and one system has retained control. For outsiders it is extremely difficult to keep tabs on who's who in the largely monolithic political structure with its messianic overtones surrounding what has come to be known as the cult of Kim, wherein the followers of Kim Il-sung—and later on, his son

Kim Jong-il—display a mixture of reverential devotion to leaders and their teachings coupled with automaton-like deference. One useful approach to assess the pecking order in North Korean society has been to use techniques developed within Kremlinology for noncommunist observers of the Soviet Union at its height. Conceptually this is worthwhile, but because of the DPRK's penchant for tight control and secrecy that verges on paranoia, this is easier said than done. North Korea's elites do not periodically line up on a North Korean version of a Kremlin wall overlooking a Red Square in ways that would permit guesstimates about who ranks where. Moreover, in contrast to South Korea's increasing openness, North Korea became less transparent over time. The various branches of North Korea's government bureaucracy are tightly regulated and those branches that might seem capable of presenting independent policy viewpoints, such as the Supreme People's Assembly, the court system, or the cabinet largely act as rubber stamps in sanctioning what the Great Leader declares to be good for Korea. Even though the Korean Workers Party is a pervasive organization, facilitating domestic espionage that helps guarantee discipline, the decision-making elite has been, and is, quite small.

The Kim dynasty became far more dynastic as a result of programmed political changes that began in the mid-1970s. These were designed to institutionalize generational succession to keep up with the passage of time, but also to provide guidance for transforming the cadre of elite advisors around the designated successor—Kim Il-sung's son, Kim Jong-il—so that their personal loyalty and fealty to the Kim line would remain intact.[2] The younger Kim, known as the "Party Center" and the "Dear Leader," was credited with all sorts of expertise comparable to his father's. In short, the cult of Kim was transferred down the lineage largely intact, albeit adjusted to meet the expectations of a younger generation of North Koreans and to take advantage of Kim Jong-il's penchant for exploring variations on his father's themes. These included Kim Jong-il's interests in systematizing the concepts in Kim Il-sung thought in ways that infused it with an almost theological quality. The younger Kim also was credited with encouraging North Korea to be more innovative in order to guide the DPRK toward reform reminiscent of Deng Xiaoping's in China. Although such efforts were well intentioned and almost certainly motivated by North Korean recognition of how much the DPRK was falling behind the ROK during the 1970s and 1980s, the DPRK's rigid political and economic system—coupled with its seriously flawed understanding of how a successful state should operate—consistently led North Korea down the path to failure.

Exactly how well prepared Kim Jong-il was to assume the mantle of revered leader from his father is very debatable. The eldest of Kim Il-sung's children, Kim Jong-il certainly had the best upbringing available in the DPRK. However, by being pampered and fawned over as the heir apparent in the Kim dynasty, his competence was not really tested in ways that could help make him a truly viable leader of a state that could be competitive in an international environment and which was experiencing the transition from the Cold War to the post–Cold War eras. The Kims, father and son, essentially were committed to institutionalizing a controlled revolutionary process via their manipulation of the factional dynamic that is endemic within the traditions of Korean political culture. However, because of the artificial qualities inherent in North Korea's rigidly controlled environment, the two Kims ended up creating a Kim dynasty that can fairly be described as a hothouse revolutionary state, which has been in danger for some time of not being able to survive when external factors threaten to shatter the hothouse glass.

Politically there has been, and is, a reasonable chance that the North Korean leadership elite can continue to prevail in the seat of power through a combination of intimidation, denial of alternative options, the almost mystical qualities surrounding the cult of Kim, and an ability to persuade followers about the correctness of the course North Korea has been on for half a century. In perverse ways that political strength may have been bolstered by a younger generation of South Koreans, who have expressed guarded respect in the twenty-first century for North Korean political resistance to U.S. pressures to reform on American terms. Nonetheless, the DPRK's economic problems and the poor ability of the political class to cope with these economic challenges are poised to shatter the hothouse environment. North Korea's economic status, compared to a spectrum of other countries, but pointedly to South Korea, has not looked good for quite a while. The comparative advantages the DPRK once enjoyed disappeared long ago. Even after North Korea rebounded from the Korean War and muddled its way through the challenges posed by the Sino-Soviet split to a level where its manipulated economic data appeared to be competitive in the late 1970s and early 1980s, its facade was damaged by the closer scrutiny provoked by South Korea's growing and widely recognized economic power and the PRC's pursuit of economic reforms that were in part influenced by the ROK's successes. The serious mismanagement of North Korea's economy, the pressure put on the economy by the cost of an enormous military establishment that the DPRK literally could not afford to maintain, wasteful priorities, and recurrent bad luck with Pyongyang's preparation for natural and manmade disasters have resulted in the DPRK slipping ever closer to collapsing, imploding, or self-destructing. In an attempt to rectify its many problems, North Korea tried to change course economically by using foreign policy leverage to obtain aid and devising revised interpretations of the Kimist *juche* doctrine, but little progress was made. This dilemma can best be explained in the context of North Korea's international relations, which shall be assessed in the remainder of this chapter.

FOREIGN AND DEFENSE POLICIES

As is true of South Korea, North Korea exhibits a split personality on the foreign policy front because of the approach it takes toward its Korean rival versus the rest of the world. As noted with regard to South Korea in chapter 5, this section also shall deal with the DPRK's approach to unification mainly in a passing context, leaving the issue primarily to the two concluding chapters. Also like South Korea, North Korea in its pre-sovereign state role could not have a formal foreign policy.

Nonetheless, and like the pre-ROK South Korean leaders' maneuvering for influence over their U.S. mentors, the pre-DPRK North Korea leaders also sought every opportunity to influence their Soviet mentors. The North Koreans, for reasons pertaining to their Soviet ties and to the Soviet occupiers' vision for the Korean peninsula, had ample reason to believe they were far more successful in shaping their mentors' perspectives on Korea. While there is ample reason to conclude that their confidence was warranted, it is also important to note that they did not face nearly as formidable a challenge as their southern counterparts in terms of their respective mentors' knowledge base regarding Korean affairs. For both Koreas, the Korean War turned out to be a foreign policy watershed. On balance, South Korea benefited far more from this watershed than North Korea. Had the DPRK not been so confident and aggressive, it might well have achieved its goals by simply waiting for the ROK to flounder around long enough for the United States to lose interest in it. Instead, the DPRK pursued policies that caused the United States to become far more committed to its Korean ally in the Cold War and perceive North Korea as one of the United States' most fanatical adversaries. Making matters still worse, North Korea's widespread image as the aggressive instigator of the Korean War permanently tarnished its reputation in the eyes of the majority of the international community. More than half a century after that watershed event, North Korea still struggles with that legacy.

Beyond that historical burden, North Korea's foreign policy has been more thoroughly marked by its inflexible domestic political and economic evolution than was the case for South Korea.[3] Over the post–Korean War decades, as the ROK's foreign policy evolved and matured in keeping with South Korea's democratic and capitalist evolution, the DPRK's relatively rigid domestic parameters set the tone for North Korea's long-term pattern in its foreign policy. The DPRK has pursued two tacts in its foreign policy, both substantially shaped by North Korean goals on the inter-Korean front. First, throughout the Cold War and even into the post–Cold War era, Pyongyang has maintained a distinct set of relationships with the Marxist world and activist groups that aspired to be part of that world. Second, Pyongyang has maintained a far more varied set of relationships with the non-socialist world—ranging from hostile relations with adversaries to fairly passive relations with other free world countries that did not take sides on the inter-Korean issues.

Because of the nature of the North Korean state and its Cold War roots, the DPRK placed overwhelming emphasis on its relationships with the Soviet Union and the People's Republic of China. Initially the preeminence of the Soviet Union in global communist affairs, as well as its role as one of Korea's liberators, compelled the DPRK to put an unequivocal priority on the USSR. Despite that necessity,

North Korea did not slip into the sort of client-state relationship with the Soviet Union that South Korea entered into with the United States because of the evolving ROK-United States security relationship. Instead, the DPRK became a different type of client in its bonds with the Soviet Union because its obligations to the USSR were tempered by the PRC's greater role in the Korean War, which offset the role of the Soviet Union. That balance was skewed even more by the emergence of the Sino-Soviet split. On the face of it, those frictions put North Korea in an awkward position where it had to acquiesce to rival pressures from these giants of the communist world. While the DPRK certainly did shift to-and-fro using a policy framework that permitted it to muddle through a troubled period, from Pyongyang's perspective it did so in a manner that permitted North Korea to manipulate, instead of being manipulated by, the rift between the two giants. Rather than being tugged between the Sino-Soviet rivals, Pyongyang perceived its position between the two as a source of leverage. In essence it was making a virtue of necessity. Because that mind-set also spawned the DPRK's *juche* philosophy of self-reliance, which became an ever more important aspect of North Korea's perception of itself compared to other countries, that mind-set has had a lasting impact on its overall foreign policy. This situation enabled North Korea to project an image of nonalignment, even if it barely fit the criteria for that category. Because North Korea came to see itself as an alternate model of socialist development guided by the revolutionary insights of Kim Il-sung thought, the DPRK has held itself out as an example for third world and nonaligned countries.

As the United States' role in East and Southeast Asia after the Korean War expanded, with its strategic anchor in Japan and the support of the ROK-United States alliance, the DPRK began to see its ability to be a thorn in the side of that U.S.-led strategic grouping as a significant asset. When the Vietnam War expanded in scope and intensity, drawing in South Korea on the U.S.-led side, North Korea saw its position regarding deterrence being enhanced by circumstances. Given the support provided to North Vietnam by the Soviet Union and the PRC, North Korea was able to get credit for supporting all three in low-key ways because each recognized that the DPRK had its hands full on the peninsula. Despite the threat that Pyongyang perceived from the United States-ROK alliance, it also understood that neither was ready to wage a renewed war in Korea while the Vietnam War was underway. In its perverse way that reinforced American and South Korean concerns about the rationality of North Korea's leaders, and thereby helped the DPRK's approach to deterrence: North Korea engaged in a series of relatively low-key DMZ provocations from 1966–1969. More visibly North Korea also directly challenged the United States by seizing a U.S. Navy intelligence-gathering ship, the USS *Pueblo*, in January 1968, and shooting down a U.S. EC-121 naval reconnaissance plane in April 1969. Since North Korean commandos also attempted a raid on the Blue House in Seoul during the same month as the *Pueblo* incident, these acts raised serious concerns about renewed war. On balance, they turned out to be provocative moves by North Korea intended to get its adversaries to take it seriously, which they did by heightening their defenses, but also by engaging in negotiations that rescued the *Pueblo*'s crew and lowered tensions for a while. Within the broader context of North Korea's foreign and defense policies these reckless acts accomplished their goals by compelling the DPRK's adversaries to take it seriously.

It also caused the two communist giants to reevaluate the rationality of the DPRK's leaders. While North Korea's provocative policies and acts were mainly focused on the perceived threat of the ROK-United States alliance to its south, Pyongyang also was sending more oblique signals to Moscow and Beijing about how independent North Korea could be. The DPRK had been troubled by the escalating tensions between the Soviet Union and the PRC that spawned a border clash in 1969. While North Korea could not avoid becoming enmeshed in the context of these tensions because of its common borders with both giants, it was determined to not become a pawn. Instead, North Korea tried to play off each one's interest in the DPRK against the other's, maximizing Pyongyang's leverage in the process. In that context Pyongyang's high-risk acts caused Moscow and Beijing to become both more critical of, and more cautious with regard to, the DPRK. This too amounted to enhanced leverage for bolstering North Korean deterrence because of the signals it conveyed that effectively reinforced a policy of calculated irrationality.

The parameters of North Korean foreign and defense policy assumptions were shaken by two major mid–Cold War events. One was the beginning of the U.S.-PRC normalization process, symbolized by the Nixon-Mao summit in February 1972, and reinforced by the Nixon Doctrine's goal of a changing U.S. role in Asia. The other was U.S.-USSR detente. Although neither came close to the truly daunting impact of the end of the Cold War and the Soviet Union's dissolution, these two turning points—compounded by the ROK's growing economic stature and international clout—caused North Korea to rethink its international stance. This rethinking process led to a limited effort to tone down the harshness of its image, including efforts in 1972 to expand the DPRK-ROK dialogue. That did not last, however, and the DPRK rapidly returned to a more provocative approach, including an August 1974 attempt to assassinate ROK President Park Chung-hee during which Park's wife was killed. Throughout the remainder of the 1970s, North Korea slipped into a more isolated stance internationally, although the DPRK expanded its support for various revolutionary groups around the world, notably in the Middle East, Africa, and Latin America.

When the Cold War became colder again during the Reagan years, North Korea did its best to cope with conflicting pressures. The DPRK benefited from the controversy surrounding the USSR's shooting down a South Korean airliner, KAL 007, in September 1983. North Korea seized upon the momentum created in that atmosphere by launching an attack on ROK officials visiting Rangoon, Burma, in October 1983, killing thirteen. The DPRK was en route to cultivating a role as what became known as a rogue state because of its support for revolutionary groups that functioned as terrorists. This image added to North Korea's deterrence capability because of the intentional way it projected a sense of irrationality. This posture was underscored again by North Korean agents in a November 1987 bombing of KAL 858 over Thailand, killing 115 people. As much as North Korea pressed forward in this manner, the course of the Cold War was not helping the DPRK's cause. Neither the advent of the Gorbachev government in Moscow, nor the PRC's role as both a de facto U.S. ally against the Soviet Union and as a country that was transforming its socioeconomic system, were in North Korea's perceived interests. Compounding this was South Korea's rapid economic growth, its enhanced international stature, symbolized by the 1988 Seoul Olympics, and the ROK's adaptation of West Germany's *Ostpolitik* policy into its *Nordpolitik* efforts to simultaneously reach out to Beijing and Moscow while undercutting Pyongyang.

The end of the Cold War was momentous for the entire world, but it was truly traumatic for North Korea because it eliminated many of the contextual realities to which Pyongyang had grown thoroughly accustomed. As a result of North Korea's deteriorating economy, its out-of-step political system, and its rogue-state international image—in addition to South Korea coming out on the winning side of the Cold War—the DPRK was a very disoriented player in the international system with poor prospects for surviving as a viable state. Considering how bleak circumstances were for North Korea at the end of the Cold War, with the Soviet Union's dissolution, Germany's unification, and great uncertainty about how the PRC would adjust to an apparent new world order, it is remarkable that the DPRK has not only survived but has managed to use these circumstances to its own advantage. The ways North Korea has brought this about are complex. On one level it has used the loss of the Soviet Union and the rise of the PRC in Asian and global affairs in creative ways. Not having a Sino-Soviet balance of powers in the background limiting the DPRK's ability to explore all its strategic options made it easier for Pyongyang to pursue its nuclear option. The fact that China had chosen that path in the mid-1960s clearly was not lost on North Korea's leadership. The PRC's economic reforms in the 1980s and 1990s also loomed large for North Korea as it faced international pressure to break away from its failed economic policies. North Korea's proximity to China, coupled with the PRC's desire to be a role model for North Korea, became a factor in North Korean foreign policy calculations.

On other levels North Korea has been able to adapt its past approach of making a virtue of necessity. This is evident in the ways the DPRK has used its admission about its impoverished status to generate sympathy in some quarters—notably among the younger generation of South Koreans. All of this was facilitated by North Korea's decision early in the post–Cold War period, September 1991, to acquiesce to international pressure, especially from Beijing, to accept the concept of joint DPRK and ROK entry into the United Nations. At the same time as the DPRK was pursuing its nuclear option, it was positioning itself to make use of its place in the United Nations in ways that were previously unavailable to the Kim regime. North Korea also has used the United Nations and all of the international attention generated by its pursuit of a nuclear option to expand the spectrum of foreign contacts available to the DPRK. This made the DPRK's foreign policy far more complex than it had been before.

At the center of all these developments, without question, is the purpose behind the DPRK's nuclear option. There are various perspectives on this issue. Most analysts are convinced that North Korea fully intended to develop nuclear weapons and the means to deliver them. To what extent they succeeded is widely debated. Other, more Machiavellian, perceptions of North Korea's intentions suspect its nuclear option always was more of a diplomatic shell game than a serious attempt to join the international nuclear club because of the palpable risks of doing so. Given North Korea's compact territory, even as a nuclear power proclaiming its effectiveness for deterrence, were the DPRK to ever actually use nuclear weapons to attack its presumed adversaries in the United States-ROK alliance, North Korea would be very vulnerable to retaliatory attacks that would obliterate it. In either case, the way in which the DPRK's pursuit of a nuclear option was discovered, brought the United States and North Korea to the cusp of war in 1994, and led to an evolving series of international negotiations and multilateral interventions—such as the Korean Peninsula Energy Development Organization (KEDO)—and became yet another instance of North Korea making a virtue of necessity. The DPRK maximized its leverage through brinkmanship diplomacy, the creative use of manipulative deterrence to play upon international anxieties about the supposed irrationality of the leadership elite in Pyongyang, and the advantageous use of its foreign and defense policy position in the context of inter-Korean relations.

Although North Korea—like South Korea—had a fairly consistent record of keeping its foreign policy on a separate track from its inter-Korean policies, the DPRK's post–Cold War use of its nuclear option blurred the line distinguishing these two tracks. Given North Korea's past negative perception of South Korean political leaders and animosity toward the ROK's international role in conjunction with the United States and Japan, it is safe to assume that Kim Jong-il and his core advisors had no expectation that Seoul might become amenable to a meaningful dialogue with Pyongyang, which would require the ROK to resist pressure from Washington and Tokyo. That assumption is supported by the fact that North Korea's perception of the threat posed by the ROK to the DPRK illustrates Pyongyang's acceptance of the geopolitical realities created by South Korea's economic power and its importance within the international economic system. This made South Korea a very different sort of "threat" to North Korea, even though the DPRK remained concerned about the military risks it faced as a result of the United States-ROK alliance. Nonetheless, the combination of South Korean pragmatic responses to the complex international circumstances generated by North Korean nuclear brinkmanship, the emergence of the Kim Dae-jung government with its Sunshine Policy agenda, and South Korea's subsequent moves toward greater liberal-progressive flexibility under the Roh Moo-hyun government with its younger generation supporters, led North Korea toward a more adaptive blending of its foreign and inter-Korean policies.

North Korea's long-term development of a more nationalist brand of domestic politics, which differentiated it from its Soviet and Chinese neighbors, and built upon the ways the Kim dynasty creatively used the political legacy of Korea's historical traditions, also proved useful in that these elements of nationalism began to strike a chord among South Korea's younger generation. North Korea's evolving use of its *juche* philosophy reinforced this by shifting North Korea's focus from the pursuit of complete self-reliance to the avoidance of abject dependence. This permitted North Korea's nationalism to mesh with South Korea's perceptions of interdependence in ways that hinted at the virtue for both Koreas' foreign policies to avoid becoming subject to excessive foreign pressure, and helped them both visualize a common future.

The impact of North and South Korean interaction within the context created by international responses to the DPRK's nuclear brinkmanship have been complicated by several factors. Foremost have been the pressures generated among countries that want to devise a solution to this problem by cooperating with each other. The

United States, in particular, has sought such cooperation with the PRC and Japan to supplement what Washington assumes will be U.S.-ROK cooperation. However, each of these countries brings different motives and perceptions to the issue. While South Korea has to appear supportive of alliance cooperation with the United States, there are complicating nuances that raise questions about the authenticity of the support. Many South Koreans perceive differences in U.S. versus South Korean interests within a supposedly joint policy on the DPRK nuclear issue. That gap is underscored by South Korean resentment about greater U.S. readiness to block Korean nuclear ambitions—the ROK in the Park years and the DPRK today—than to block Japanese nuclear potentials. Differing U.S.-ROK views on how to best handle North Korean nuclear brinkmanship also were complicated by Seoul's unhappiness over the Bush administration's post-9/11 use of the "axis of evil" metaphor to link North Korea to potential Middle Eastern nuclear threats and the Bush doctrine's advocacy of a preemptive strike strategy that could be applied to North Korea. From Pyongyang's vantage point, these U.S.-ROK differences provided an opportunity to make a foreign policy point about U.S. double standards and the risks inherent in U.S. post-9/11 policies, a point which was calculated to send signals to anyone in South Korea and the rest of the world who doubted the soundness of U.S. policy to take another look at North Korea's policies.

American efforts to bolster U.S.-Japanese cooperation vis-à-vis North Korean nuclear brinkmanship tended to be more effective than efforts aimed at U.S.-ROK cooperation. In part this was due to internal Japanese factors centered on a revived debate about Japan's proper defense policy. When North Korean provocations, such as using its naval forces near Japan and testing a missile over Japan, were seen as spin-offs of the brinkmanship policy that went too far, Japan responded by being unilaterally ready to lash out at North Korea and bilaterally ready to cooperate more thoroughly with the United States in devising means to resolve the problems caused by North Korea's use of a nuclear option. Although this situation clearly complicated the DPRK's foreign policy agenda, it also created additional opportunities for Pyongyang to make use of differences between Tokyo and Seoul as partners of Washington and to use ROK and PRC anxieties about what a stronger Japanese military reaction might mean for each of them. North Korea is well aware that China and South Korea are wary of the prospect of revived Japanese militarism causing problems for Asia's future. Once again North Korea was able to use a factor that was widely perceived as negative to the DPRK in creative ways as positive leverage.

Perhaps the most convoluted mix of factors has been China's reactions and their usefulness for North Korea. As much as the PRC has worked with the United States, the ROK, and Japan in the contexts just outlined, it also has pressed its own perspectives on how China can play a central role in inducing North Korea to change course and why both Koreas can look to China for help in resolving the nuclear issue in ways that they cannot expect from the United States or Japan. China's existing roles in this issue have been guardedly welcomed by the United States or Japan, but its potential roles in the future cause concern in some quarters of Washington and Tokyo. Here, too, this combination of factors has created opportunities for North Korea's foreign policy. Given the DPRK's past relations with the PRC, North Korea has solid reasons to hope that China will not sell it out. Moreover, given China's overall history with all of Korea, with Japan, and with the United States, there is reason for North Koreans—as simply Koreans—to be optimistic that China can be relied upon more than Japan or the United States to do what is best for Sino-Korean interests. This facilitates the ways North Korea can make use of Chinese desires to play a central role vis-à-vis Korea in the DPRK's foreign policy toward the United States and Japan, as well as within Pyongyang's approach to the inter-Korean relationship.

Further complicating North and South Korean interactions, in the context of these countries' reactions to DPRK's nuclear brinkmanship, is the impact of Kim Jong-il's post-9/11 relationship with President Bush. As the head of a state lumped by President Bush into the "axis of evil," and knowing that President Bush has described Kim as a "pygmy" and said he "loathed" Kim, there is virtually no doubt about how Kim Jong-il would characterize President Bush. Although South Korean officials' recognition of the importance of the ROK-United States alliance in coping with North Korea and resolving outstanding issues—especially the nuclear problem—will require the ROK to avoid any harsh statements about President Bush or any other U.S. president, it is evident in the anti-American sentiments expressed by quite a few South Korean pundits and supporters of President Roh Moo-hyun that they might personally characterize President Bush and his policies in a similarly negative manner. Once again circumstances have presented North Korea with an opportunity to use a wedge issue in creative ways in its foreign policy.

All of these developments point to what amounts to creative North Korean diplomacy. Pyongyang makes the best of bad situations by playing on adversaries' concerns about the circumstances becoming worse if measures are not taken to address North Korea's needs and aspirations. This enables the DPRK to maneuver for concessions in exchange for North Korean cooperation. It also helps North Korea to use its tensions with the United States and Japan in roughly the same ways as it did amidst Sino-Soviet attempts to manipulate the DPRK, trying to use each one's pressure on the DPRK to North Korea's advantage by turning it into viable leverage within inter-Korean relations. Pyongyang does this by using separate and joint U.S. and Japanese responses to North Korean nuclear brinkmanship to bolster the DPRK's prospects for establishing bilateral diplomatic ties with Washington and Tokyo. It has enjoyed some success. On the U.S. front there have been several working-level bilateral meetings, but no summit meetings. However, on the Japanese front there have been considerably more working-level meetings, but—more importantly—two summit meetings between Kim Jong-il and Prime Minister Koizumi Junichiro, in 2002 and 2004. These efforts are useful to North Korean foreign policy in terms of improving its image and because they could produce positive results on the nuclear issue. However, they also are important for inter-Korean relations because of the way they seize opportunities stemming from the circumstances created by South Korea's *Nordpolitik* policy. In short, this enables North Korea to build the bilateral networks that South Korea deems necessary for both Koreas to participate in productive multilateral relationships that will facilitate gradual improvement in inter-Korean attempts to reconcile their differences.

As noted above, trend lines in North and South Korea's existing policies that encourage overlapping approaches to not being subjected to excessive foreign pressures may lead them to perceive a common future. These aspects of North Korea's and South Korea's future policies toward each other and how they may be perceived internationally clearly shall have consequences for the international system and a potentially unified Korea. This shall be addressed in the remaining chapters. To conclude this chapter on North Korea's domestic political and economic evolution and the consequences for its foreign and defense policies, it is worthwhile emphasizing that no one—not even Kim Jong-il with the aura of greatness and insight ascribed to him within the cult of Kim—has a crystal ball than can predict the DPRK's future for as long as it remains a separate state in a divided Korean nation. While the DPRK may manage to persist as a rigid political entity with a flawed economy and a reckless international role, this seems unlikely. Past forecasts about North Korea's demise have not been accurate. Nonetheless, to most observers, the fact that the DPRK has lasted so long is no guarantee that it will be able to continue to persist using the same means. It is far more likely that the DPRK will have to accept the need to transform itself either to last as a separate state or to set the stage for a transition to a new Korea that will want to draw on some of the political, economic, and international legacies created by the DPRK for however long it is able to last. In this sense, North Korea's achievements as a separate state probably will not prove to be as important as South Korea's for overall Korea, when future Korean historians many years from now look back upon the period Korea was a divided nation in the twentieth and twenty-first centuries. But North Korea's leaders almost certainly will do as much as they can to assure that their legacy shall remain embedded and appreciated for eternity.

CHAPTER 7

Two Koreas: International Perspectives

The two Koreas have been entangled in international affairs since their creation as separate states. Over time the major powers with a significant stake in the Korean peninsula—the United States, the Soviet Union/Russia, the People's Republic of China, and Japan—have all matured in their relations with both Koreas. All four countries' policies have evolved significantly since the early years described in chapter 4. Beyond these major powers, a spectrum of other international players have developed interests in Korean affairs. This chapter shall address each of these relationships.

UNITED STATES–KOREA RELATIONS

U.S. policy toward the two Koreas was compelled by the Cold War and the Korean War to take sides regarding the two Koreas in ways that persist to this day. The United States-ROK alliance and socioeconomic partnership has evolved with changing U.S. and South Korean interests. Similarly the adversarial relationship between the United States and the DPRK has been transformed by circumstances.

Clearly the Korean War was the watershed event in U.S.-ROK relations. The U.S. stake in Korea was fundamentally changed via the bond of blood created by that war's casualties. After the war, the U.S. client-mentor relationship with the Syngman Rhee regime made a difficult transition into the sequence of military-backed authoritarian regimes during the Park, Chun, and Roh years. The reasons the United States and its UN allies waged the Korean War on behalf of a democratically free Korea were undercut by the Park coup and the nearly three decades of military-linked governments, albeit elected, which followed. This political divide was softened by the economic successes enjoyed by South Korea throughout the 1960s, 1970s, and 1980s—drawing on both a U.S.-influenced Western-style capitalist model as well as a Japanese Confucian-influenced capitalist model—which brought the U.S.-ROK relationship into greater harmony through another brand of client-mentor interaction. The 1960s and early 1970s also contributed to the United States-ROK alliance because of the United States' need for allies to join its military effort in Vietnam. The contributions of the ROK's armed forces to that cause also bolstered South Korea's economy via the corollary networking and further strengthened the U.S.-ROK relationship.

While the U.S. government became even more well disposed toward the ROK during those years, and cultivated a cadre of American experts on Korea to make U.S. policy more effective, which symbolized the perceived importance South Korea was acquiring for the United States, other American experts in Korean affairs began to explore dissenting views of what the United States should do regarding both its Korean ally and adversary.[1] This plurality of U.S. views was, and is, significant because it embodied the growing debate within the United States about what is most appropriate for U.S. policy toward both Koreas as the circumstances on the peninsula evolve via a more prosperous and maturing South Korea versus a more stagnant and "rogue" North Korea.

The causes behind U.S. frictions with South Korea also evolved over the years. During the Carter administration, human rights controversies loomed large. While that issue faded during the Reagan and G.H.W. Bush years, bilateral economic frictions grew due to U.S. resistance to South Korea's shortcomings in free market trade, which amounted to protectionism. Seoul's manipulation of popular anti-American responses to U.S. pressures for reform exacerbated that situation. Mitigating such frictions in the post-Carter years were conservative ideological bonds between the Reagan-Bush administrations and the Chun-Roh administrations that, coupled with the ROK's growing foreign policy sophistication during those years, which made South Korea less overtly dependent upon the United States, facilitated the U.S.-ROK maturation process. Concurrently, the Reagan era's intensification of the Cold War—reinforced by growing U.S.-PRC ties ever since the Nixon administration—which ultimately led to the collapse of the Soviet Union and end of the Cold War, had a huge impact on overall U.S.-Korea relations. It reinforced the United States-ROK alliance by putting South Korea on the prevailing side of the conflict, and it aggravated the adversarial ties between the United States and the DPRK by worsening North Korea's situation as the Cold War unraveled.

Early in the post–Cold War era, the Gulf War success of the G.H.W. Bush administration compounded the signals being sent to North Korea about what kind of threat it faced. Although the Bush and early Clinton years also were focused on the possibility of an international "peace dividend" stemming from the Cold War's end, in ways that caused some anxiety about the prospects of the United States-ROK alliance if U.S. forces were to be cut, that was more than offset by the way North Korea was attempting to deal with the post–Cold War era by exploring its nuclear options. Because of the ways President Clinton's "new Democrat" paradigm and his "comeback kid" image represented an political model for some key South Korean leaders—notably Kim Young-sam and Kim Dae-jung—the Clinton years had the potential to be very positive in terms of the impact of U.S. policy on Korea. However, as the DPRK's nuclear ambitions erupted, U.S. policy toward both Koreas was seriously influenced.

Partly because U.S. policy in the post–Cold War era was in search of a new international purpose and partly because of the Clinton administration's commitment to Wilsonian activist internationalism, as demonstrated in Bosnia and Kosovo, the United States was strongly committed to an antinuclear proliferation agenda. This put the United States on a collision course with North Korea's aspirations that nearly led to U.S. military action against the DPRK in the spring of 1994, which was averted through various diplomatic measures, including former President Jimmy Carter's private mission to

Pyongyang in June of 1994. Even though what the United States was doing to cope with North Korea was significantly in support of the United States' obligations to South Korea under the United States-ROK alliance, the way the United States reached its decisions and then carried them out caused considerable consternation among many South Koreans. Too much of what the United States did toward Korea seemed to be the result of U.S. global interests in antiproliferation issues and less because of the perspectives of American experts in Korean affairs or because of meaningful close consultations between Washington and Seoul. As controversial as U.S. policy toward North Korea's nuclear option was among South Koreans, the negotiation procedures devised by the United States through the Korean Peninsula Energy Development Organization (KEDO), through multilateral fora such as the Six-Party Talks (United States, China, Japan, Russia, and the two Koreas) and United States-Japan-ROK trilateral talks, and the turn to the United Nations to help tone down North Korea's aggressive potentials, only partly mollified South Korean critics but aggravated some American conservative critics who lambasted the whole effort as appeasement.

The switch from the Clinton to the G. W. Bush administration compounded these frictions. The Bush team's desire for a tougher policy toward North Korea were intensified by its negative perceptions of the Kim Dae-jung administration's Sunshine Policy as grossly naive. This compounding process was worsened by the 9/11 terrorist attacks, by President Bush's inclusion of North Korea in an "axis of evil" during his 1992 State of the Union Address to Congress, and by South Korea's replacement of DJ with Roh Moo-hyun as its president. The U.S.-ROK relationship was marked by Roh's aversion to knuckling under to any form of U.S. hegemony and his supporters' anti-American sentiment and disdain for Bush. President Bush's overt "loathing" of Kim Jong-il added to this mix. The United States' hard-line posture toward North Korea favored regime change and attempted to build international coercive pressure on North Korea to acquiesce on the nuclear issue. This entire situation was under close scrutiny as a result of the United States' Global War on Terrorism (GWOT) with its pressure on allies—such as South Korea—to get on board, and with questions about the appropriateness of U.S. priorities regarding those who possess weapons of mass destruction (WMD). When WMD as the rationale for war in Iraq came up short, the Bush administration found itself in a very awkward position regarding North Korea. Since the DPRK used its nuclear option as a form of deterrence against the United States, the logic of a preemptive attack seemed plausible to some. None of this was helped by the controversies surrounding U.S. pressure on Seoul to help the military coalition in Iraq, by South Korea's concerns about the impact of U.S. armed forces' global transformation measures leading to force cuts within the bilateral alliance, and by South Korea's readiness to explore diplomatic alternatives proffered by countries such as China.

Neither South Korea's liberal leaders nor North Korea's very hard-line regime were supportive of President George W. Bush's reelection in 2004. Nonetheless, the ROK quickly adjusted to the reality of a second Bush term that would coincide with the remainder of President Roh's term in office, and sought to keep the ROK-United States alliance on a viable track. Predictably North Korea was more hostile toward the Bush administration's hard-line WMD pressures on the DPRK and its intensified agenda to export freedom and democracy worldwide, which clearly targeted North Korea, characterized by Washington as an "outpost of tyranny." North Korea's adverse reaction to having to cope with the Bush administration for four more years complicated South Korea's relations with U.S.-DPRK relations and the policies of both China and Japan toward that difficult relationship.

Looming in the background of all this have been concerns in South Korea about its U.S. ally's readiness to be cooperative on the sensitive issue of Korean unification. All too many Koreans in the South increasingly share with their northern brethren a view of the United States as not really supportive of a peacefully negotiated inter-Korean reconciliation and unification agenda. The United States is perceived as either supportive of the status quo of a divided Korean nation because it serves existing U.S. national interests and those of its main ally in Asia, namely Japan, or as ready to foster North Korean regime change in ways that would enable Washington to guide the post-collapse situation to the United States' advantage in the region. This issue is, and is likely to remain, a major facet of U.S. policy toward Korea until the issue is resolved. How that may be achieved shall be examined from a Korean perspective in the next chapter.

RUSSIA-KOREA RELATIONS

Contemporary Russian relations with the two Koreas are clearly derived from Czarist Russia's nineteenth-century involvement and mid-twentieth-century Soviet involvement in the Korean peninsula. For better or worse, and examples of both exist, Russians played a major role in how Koreans got entangled in the imperial maneuvering that put them under Japan's wing, only to be liberated as a soon-to-be-divided nation. Strikingly unlike the post–World War II Americans who dealt with Korea, the Russians cannot be accused of lacking a vision for Korea's future. Unfortunately for the Korean people in both halves of what would become a divided entity, the Russian vision for Korea rapidly put it at odds with the United States, and provided what would prove to be a fatally flawed political and economic model for its North Korean protégé. This compounded the longer term inter-Korean tensions as a result of the Sino-Soviet regional tensions that divided the DPRK's loyalties.

The Soviet Union's initial ability to be a benefactor for North Korea was aided by collective Korean memories of the positive legacies of Czarist Russia's willingness to stand up to an expansionist Japan and by the ways the USSR helped Marxist Asians from China and Korea wage a resistance struggle against the Japanese oppressor. Many Koreans who escaped from Japanese-controlled Korea and Manchuria found their way to the Soviet Union, where they absorbed the Soviet worldview. This made it much easier for the USSR to have its vision of postwar Korea accepted by many Koreans. Had the Cold War not erupted, and had the PRC not emerged in ways that positioned it to help North Korea as it did during the Korean War, it is virtually certain that the Soviet plan for Korea would have prevailed for as long as the Soviet Union might have lasted. Of course those are two daunting hypotheticals, neither of which came close to being realized.

Both the Cold War and the Korean War altered the Soviet vision for the Korean peninsula. The United States' response in the Korean situation changed the world for the Soviet Union, pointing out the challenge Moscow would face and giving it an opportunity to test the geopolitical waters. Although China's entry into the Korean War structurally aided the Soviet-led cause regionally, it rapidly conveyed conflicting signals about Soviet resolve. While the Soviet Union supported North Korea's actions, it did not formally commit any forces to the war—lest it escalate to a confrontation with the United States. For North Koreans this put the USSR and the PRC into different categories. Even though the DPRK remained ideologically in tune with the Soviet Union for long enough to put a decidedly Leninist-Stalinist stamp on the North Korean system, the DPRK-PRC wartime blood bond became akin to the United States-ROK alliance ties and led leaders in Pyongyang and Beijing to refer to it as a "lips and teeth" relationship. By the late 1950s and early 1960s, North Korea found itself in the middle of Sino-Soviet tensions that proved to be a problem for the Soviet Union as the DPRK experimented with playing off one side against the other from the 1960s through the end of the Cold War.

As Sino-Soviet tensions and border frictions grew over the years, especially after U.S.-PRC normalization of relations from the Nixon to Carter administrations gave China an incentive to become a de facto adjunct to a U.S.-led array of allies across Eurasia from NATO to Japan, Soviet appreciation for the potential importance of the DPRK grew. Moscow appreciated North Korea's utility as a border state in Northeast Asia and as a key to maintaining the status quo on the Korean peninsula that helped to keep the United States preoccupied in that region. The Gorbachev era, late in the Soviet Union's history, proved to be decisive in Soviet relations with the two Koreas,[2] as declining Soviet tensions with the United States put Moscow in a position to explore its options with South Korea before, during, and after the 1988 Olympics, which drew so much international attention to the ROK, and to become more supportive of an inter-Korean dialogue process. This was better received in South Korea, which sensed that its side in the Cold War was beginning to prevail, than in North Korea, where the reorientation of both the PRC and the Soviet Union had become disconcerting in terms of the DPRK's perception of global communism. Both Koreas also recognized that these incremental changes by the Soviet Union, yielding dual recognition, were in tune with South Korea's *Nordpolitik* agenda.

The approach taken by Gorbachev toward the Korean peninsula, including the Soviet Union's formal diplomatic recognition of the ROK in September 1990 in the wake of a widely publicized summit between Gorbachev and Roh Tae-woo in San Francisco three months prior to the normalization agreement, became part of the process that led to the end of the Cold War. That issue had truly major repercussions for post–Cold War Russian relations with the DPRK as compared to South Korea. Because part of South Korea's *Nordpolitik* motive was to encourage international circumstances that would generate inter-Korean progress comparable to what occurred in Germany, one of its goals was to create an incentive for North Korea to pursue institutional reforms. The prospects for that were fairly dim at the outset because of North Korea's rigidity, but it became even worse when North Korean leaders saw the results for the Soviet Union of Gorbachev's efforts. In short, North Korean leaders were adamant about their mission to prevent the emergence of a North Korean "Gorby." They did not want the Soviet Union's fate to befall the DPRK. In that context, the more post–Cold War Russia engaged with a spectrum of capitalist countries, pointedly including South Korea that was initially enthusiastic about the economic opportunities that appeared to be latent in Russia, the more wary North Korea became of maintaining ties with the successor to its former Soviet benefactor.

Partly because Russian post–Cold War internal political and economic restructuring did not achieve rapid progress, leading to a significant decline in Russia's regional geopolitical clout, in the remainder of the 1990s and so far in the early twenty-first century, Russia's ability to be a major player in influencing the status of the Korean peninsula has eroded. However, it certainly has not disappeared. Under the Yeltsin and Putin governments, Russia has made the best of its Northeast Asian and Siberian proximity to both Koreas in terms of exports of raw materials, cooperation on maritime and land-transport connections—including the latter's implications for aiding Korean unification, and working as closely as it can with both Koreas' other neighbors and interested counterparts in the Pacific Basin, to be perceived as a useful partner. Part of the reason this approach has enjoyed considerable success is Russia's territorial links to Korea and Koreans' awareness that this geographical connection makes Russia one country away from an array of European and Central Asian states positioned on its western borders. Even though the distances are considerable, the network it suggests gives the Korean peninsula a continental linkage to a far-flung set of countries. This could become still more significant for Korea, if Russia ever became part of the expanding European Union.

Beyond that spatial connection, Russia's size and potential for resurgence as a great power remains widely recognized worldwide. In the Korean context, this provides Russia with leverage to work closely with the United States, China, and Japan on issues of common regional concern that affect Korea, but most specifically to be part of the ongoing series of Six-Party Talks addressing North Korea's nuclear option, talks which have major significance for both Koreas and for the prospects for any progress on inter-Korean reconciliation. While China, as the host of those talks and a country with better economic and security ties to both Koreas than Russia now enjoys, possesses more clout than Russia does, Russians still possess significant political and cultural assets. Drawing on Russia's nineteenth-century historical legacy of being a useful intermediary, and not having taken advantage of Korea, Russians are able to engage in dialogues with Koreans without arousing much Korean anxiety about ulterior motives. While applicable to various aspects of Russia's relations with both Koreas—including North Koreans now that their sensitivity to Russian shifts in the late 1980s and early 1990s has faded a bit—this issue is most salient when it comes to Russia's attitudes toward Korean unification. This is because Russia seems to have far less reason to resist the prospect of a reunified Korea than the United States, China, or Japan. That issue shall be addressed in greater detail in the next chapter.

CHINA-KOREA RELATIONS

As important for the two Koreas as their relationships with the United States and Russia have been, are, and will be, there is little doubt that their relationship with China—past, present, and future—looms larger. In the historical and cultural sense noted in previous chapters, the reasons for this relationship are obvious to all observers. However, China's evolving role with the two Koreas of a post–World War II era is not at all obvious and shall be examined here.[3]

Since the People's Republic of China did not yet exist when the Soviet Union and the United States played such central roles in the division of the Korean nation after its liberation from Japan, the PRC formally escapes responsibility for sanctioning that division. This is important for the PRC's subsequent contacts with both Koreas and for its potential ties with a reunified Korea. It also is important for the PRC as a nation with a perception of Taiwan as an offshore piece of China, and thus their history as a divided nation caused by the same type of Cold War–era geopolitical frictions. This vantage point, when coupled with the Chinese communists' sense of obligation to all those anti-Japanese activists from Korea who joined with the communist revolutionary cause to create the PRC, led the leaders in Beijing to perceive inherent logic in the Soviet Union's postwar vision for Korea. Consequently the PRC's role in support of the DPRK in the Korean War was consistent with its sense of duty and solidarity in an ideological environment, but it also was in keeping with China's traditional hierarchical role vis-à-vis neighboring Korea.

Had the Soviet vision for Korea preempted the eruption of the Korean War, or had the PRC's intervention in that war on behalf of that Marxist vision enabled the DPRK to prevail over the ROK and its backers, China's overall post–World War II role vis-à-vis Korea would have been entirely different. However, given the course of events that transpired after Beijing decided to intervene in the Korean War to help the DPRK and to protect PRC borders, the PRC found itself committed to one half of a bitterly divided Korean peninsula after a stalemated conflict in China's geopolitical front yard. Moreover, that course of events also reinforced the Republic of China (ROC) in Taiwan's role in the U.S.-led anticommunist coalition in the Asian theater of the Cold War. In short, the PRC was in the forefront of a major sector of that global competition. Ironically, many in the noncommunist camp perceived the PRC as an instrument of Soviet policies. While there was some accuracy in those perceptions, China's role in the Korean War and other aspects of its Maoist vision of Marxism in world affairs rapidly contributed to the emergence of a Sino-Soviet rift that gradually escalated throughout the late 1950s and 1960s—a rift which included China's development of nuclear weapons by 1964 and an armed border conflict on the Ussuri River in 1969. In that environment, China's policies toward the two Koreas remained relatively steadfast in terms of describing PRC-DPRK relations in a "lips and teeth" manner and treating South Korea as a lackey of the United States. That comparison was especially salient for China in the context of PRC-DPRK support for North Vietnam in its war against the U.S.-led coalition supporting South Vietnam that included sizable ROK forces sent by a military-backed South Korean regime. This was particularly acute when China was going through its most extremely Maoist phases, using motivational campaigns like the Great Leap Forward from 1958–1961, but especially during the various forms of its Cultural Revolution from 1965–1976. These posed unique problems for PRC-DPRK relations because each saw itself in puritanical Marxist terms, but each's brand of extremism differed significantly from the other's. In this setting, with the Soviet Union juxtaposed in opposition, the DPRK was able to try to balance its relations with each communist superpower to North Korea's advantage. The PRC's reaction to that response was to be creative in playing China's cultural cards with the North Koreans, who often could not relate as easily with most Soviet leaders' non-Asian sense of national identity.

Gradually all of that began to change, after China started to adapt to international pressure in the late 1970s, facilitated by the internal political changes fostered by Mao Tse-tung's death in 1976. This process started under Mao, when the PRC developed more flexible ties with the United States during the Nixon administration, but it accelerated during the Carter years and after. In large part this reflected China's reevaluation of the U.S.-USSR balance of power in the Cold War, which posed the larger threat to the PRC, and how China could best enhance its own capabilities. This led China to become increasingly cooperative with the Western camp of the Cold War and to move toward serious economic reforms that would expand market-based influences. These factors had major consequences for Sino-Korean relations. Although the DPRK and the PRC maintained the essence of their relations, North Korean leaders became increasingly uncertain about the wisdom of China's stance. While that increased North Korea's interest in the Soviet Union, that alternative eventually unraveled for Pyongyang when the Cold War and the Soviet Union dissolved. PRC relations with the ROK took an entirely different course. On the strategic level, China's views of the ROK shifted toward a somewhat greater understanding of their overlapping late–Cold War interests. Far more significantly, PRC leaders began to look to South Korea's economic development experiences to learn lessons applicable to China's aspirations. While the PRC was far more reluctant to acknowledge any use of either Japan or Taiwan as a de facto economic model for its national reforms, leaders in Beijing were more obviously drawing upon the experiences of earlier South Korean authoritarian regimes' use of state-guided market-based economic reforms.

In the post–Cold War era, the PRC followed the Russian precedent and diplomatically recognized the ROK in September 1992, after Seoul took the initiative to sever the ROK's once-solid formal ties with Taiwan. China had set the stage for this switch by putting pressure on North Korea to accept the concept of both Koreas being admitted to the United Nations, rather than South Korea having a unilateral move to join the UN be accepted. This pressure led to both Koreas joining the UN General Assembly in September 1991. This transition proved to be very important for China's ties to both Koreas and its influence over Korea's prospects. In part because of the way North Korea manipulated its nuclear option in a reckless manner that rejected the position of the UN-linked International Atomic Energy Agency (IAEA), thereby intensifying U.S. and Japanese anxieties, and in turn making South Korea nervous about what the other two members of the so-called virtual triangle—composed of the United States and its two Northeast Asian allies—might do in response, these circumstances created an evolving opportunity for China to exert a calming influence on all concerned. While this began during the Clinton era of U.S. policy, it accelerated during the G. W. Bush years due to his tougher foreign policy and strategic lines that imbued China's stance with the appearance of moderation. This has been underlined by China's prominent role in the Six-Party Talks, which seek a peaceful solution to the nuclear problem and are hosted in Beijing.

As important as China's role in the inter-Korean nuclear issue was, and is, the PRC also benefited greatly from the ways its burgeoning economy functioned like a magnet in attracting South Korean corporate and government interest. Along with the United States and Japan, China joined the ranks of South Korea's top-tier economic partners. As important, the ROK occupied a comparable niche for the PRC. The PRC-ROK relationship also expanded to military-to-military contacts, and considerable popular South Korean interest in China's language and culture. Although this metaphor should not be overused, China was reasserting some aspects of its traditionally important role for Korea in the eyes of many South Koreans. While the realities of PRC-DPRK relations in these realms were far short of PRC-ROK ties, after the demise of the Soviet Union, the DPRK had no real choice other than to restore the priorities formerly assigned to its "lip and teeth" senior cohort. Clearly China was not the kind of Marxist behemoth it once was, but its market-oriented societal reforms, which accelerated the PRC's climb up to becoming a strong regional power and aspiring global power, made it obvious to North Korean leaders that the PRC's role vis-à-vis the Korean peninsula would be crucial. For North Korea, the PRC had become a role model of sorts for some type of structural reform—assuming the North Korean leadership could figure out a way to pursue such a goal without losing control of their authority.

In short, China had reestablished a modern variation of its traditional role regarding Korea. The PRC's ties to both Koreas and its potential role in helping to reconfigure a single Korean nation-state, and earning its gratitude in the process of doing so, gave China greatly enhanced stature in the eyes of both Koreas. Lest this situation be overstated, it is also important to note that both Koreas were seriously upset by the way China in the early 2000s permitted some of its scholarly pundits to expound upon the possibility that the ancient Koguryo kingdom might well have been more Chinese than Korean, a not-so-subtle way to send a signal to both Koreas that—were they to become one nation-state again—they should never entertain any recidivist notions about claiming formerly Koguryo territories on the other side of the Yalu River that now are part of the PRC. Were Koreans to ever attempt such a geopolitical ploy, China has essentially told them that it could turn the tables and claim a chunk of the northern portion of the peninsula. Fortunately neither of these options is likely to ever be pursued, but by raising the issue in this manner, China has informed the Koreans about the nature of the pecking order in which Koreans will find themselves. Although Koreans presumably understand to their core that this is just one of its proverbial "whales" letting Koreans know how much it weighs, they also know it is in their larger interests to continue to improve their ties with China because of its many assets and virtues, as a way to hedge their bets with regard to the United States and Russia, and because the other "whale"—Japan—sends more worrisome signals to many Koreans.

JAPAN-KOREA RELATIONS

Of the four major powers with a significant stake in Korean affairs, there is ample evidence that Japan's relations with Korea have been the most problematic from a Korean perspective. The colonial legacy has instilled a deeply rooted distrust of Japan among many Koreans, as exemplified by the early postwar saying noted in chapter 4 warning about Japan rising again and the ways in which this attitude remains salient to this day. Nonetheless, from a Japanese vantage point, there are reasons to see Korea from a more balanced perspective.[4]

The essence of the case many Japanese make regarding Japan's relations with both Koreas is that all too many Koreans have misunderstood Japan's motives in dealing with Korea in the past and in the present. Foremost in that regard is the deep-seated Korean animosity toward Japan dating from the imperial age for undertaking measures intended to help Korean reformers. When recalling that era, Koreans recoil from the memories passed along through the generations of being victimized, oppressed, and manipulated by Japanese who claimed to be doing good deeds, while all too many Japanese—from a Korean perspective—tend to view Koreans as ingrates who cannot bring themselves to appreciate the various ways Japan facilitated the Korean nation's escape from antiquated ways and accelerated its modernization. The irony of this situation is that both arguments have some validity. Nonetheless, the gap created by these perspectives and the fervor with which so many Koreans adhere to their viewpoints makes Japan's relations with both Koreas very difficult.

Given Korean perceptions of its two neighboring "whales," in striking contrast to China's major role in the process that shaped the two Koreas in the late 1940s and early 1950s, Japan during its U.S. occupation and in the immediate aftermath was firmly on an American leash that formally precluded Japan from doing the kinds of things China did regarding Korea. Nonetheless, from a Korean—North or South—vantage point, being on the receiving end of U.S. policy toward Korea, it was clear that American officials in Washington and Tokyo were being influenced by the United States' role in reconstructing postwar Japan, by Japan's crucial geopolitical location in offshore Asia, and by Japan's reservoir of experiences in Korea that enabled U.S. policy makers to draw upon Japanese expertise in Korean issues. This is not to suggest that Japan actively pursued such a role in shaping U.S. policies toward Korea. To the extent it occurred, it was largely the result of American inexperience with Korean affairs and postwar muddling through pragmatism. However, from a Korean vantage point, it was all too easy to detect Japanese manipulation of U.S. officials to guide the United States toward devising and implementing policies that would serve Japan's interests.

Much of what the United States did in and for South Korea clearly did help postwar Japan in terms of keeping communist territorial expansionism from extending across the waters to the Japanese archipelago. As the Cold War took shape, Japan benefited by becoming the United States' cornerstone of an Asian security system that encompassed Korea. This role provided Japan's territorial security without Tokyo having to contribute very much to the task. Given Japanese society's proven sophistication in economics and the science and technology that supports commercial activities, Japan quickly became the foundation of U.S. efforts to spread a capitalist alternative to communism throughout Cold War Asia. In short, Japan benefited tremendously by being on the United States' Cold War frontier in Northeast Asia and having the United States perform many of the tasks vis-à-vis the Soviet Union, China, and Korea that the Japanese would normally have had to do for themselves. In terms of the two Koreas' views of Japan, all of this reinforced their suspicions about Japan's manipulation of circumstances pertaining to Korea for its own advantage.

During the Korea War, Japan played a crucial basing function, benefited tremendously in terms of the war's spillover effect on Japan's economic recovery, and used the Korean War's role in intensifying the Cold War to accelerate the end of the U.S. occupation and restoration of Japanese sovereignty. Japan played a very limited direct role in the Korean War, which was focused on shipping and logistics. Its post–World War II pacifism—facilitated by the U.S. occupation—enabled Japan to abstain from any fighting in the Korean War, although the war atmosphere did accelerate Japan's creation of national Self Defense Forces under U.S. pressure. In contrast to China's active intervention, Japan's policies fit a decidedly noninterventionist paradigm. In the early post–Korean War years, Japan's foreign policy was overtly focused on economic expansionism and keeping a low-profile politically. It also was profoundly risk averse. All of these criteria made Japan more than happy to leave Korea's prickly problems as much as possible in U.S. hands. In the process Japan perceived the United States as a buffer regarding the Korean peninsula, enabling Japan to be very selective in what it would and would not do. That pattern became an essential constraint in Japan's policies toward both Koreas and remains at the core of those policies to the present time.

Japan's desire to keep its distance from troublesome Korean problems was facilitated by Syngman Rhee's disdain for Japan, making the United States' dual-alliance relationship in Northeast Asia very dual—with little prospect of a meaningful third leg in that triangle. Similarly, Kim Il-sung's North Korea openly expressed its hatred of Japan's legacy and its support for U.S. policies toward North Korea. This situation was altered during the 1960s with the advent of the Park Chung-hee government. Park's willingness to adapt the Japanese economic development model to South Korea's agenda was strengthened by his reasons for responding to U.S. pressure on the ROK to improve its relationship with Japan. In turn, this created a low-risk opportunity for Japan to establish closer ties to South Korea on the economic front, which swiftly led to bilateral diplomatic ties in 1965. As important, from Japan's perspective, was South Korea's acceptance of a Japanese development model and its desire to become part of a Japan-centered expanding free market system in Asia. This was significant in the ways it indirectly affirmed Japanese views of having in the past been committed to Korean modernization. In this environment Japan-ROK commercial relations blossomed and improved bilateral political ties, which had long-term consequences for South Korean domestic politics, but this stopped far short of any direct strategic ties. While Japan offered rhetorical support for U.S. strategic activities in Korea as part of the Vietnam War–era Nixon Doctrine, and in terms of the 1969 Nixon-Sato summit where Japan acknowledged Korea's importance to Japan's security, in practical terms Japan had no genuine security obligations regarding Korea.

Moreover, Japan was not comfortable with the military-backed ROK regime's use of authoritarian measures, which reminded many Japanese of their country's militarist past. This was a sensitive issue because of the impact President Park's military education in the Japanese era probably had on his authoritarian political policies. In this context South Korean opposition groups found supporters in Japan. Perhaps the best example of this was Kim Dae-jung's anti-Park campaign in Japan which led to his kidnapping in August 1973, and which, in turn, soured Japan-ROK relations for a while. On balance, however, the economic developments noted above improved Japan's overall relations with Korea from the perspective of the two countries that mattered most to Tokyo vis-à-vis the peninsula, the United States and the ROK, but it made Japan-DPRK relations much worse because it confirmed Pyongyang's understanding of Japan's manipulative policies.

Despite Japanese diplomatic efforts to improve relations with North Korea in the 1970s, and the way the Japanese government allowed pro–North Korean activists in Japan, activists who belonged to a group called *Chosen soren* (*Chosun chongryun* in Korean), to financially support the DPRK with funds from their businesses, Japan-DPRK relations remained sour. That remained true throughout the late–Cold War years as Japan coped with the transition from Carter-era U.S.-ROK tensions—which caused concerns for Tokyo about the stability of a U.S. buffer role in Korean strategic stability—to the Reagan-Bush era's pursuit of Cold War closure, which reaffirmed the buffer for Japan. Within that same time frame, South Korea diversified its concept of security by placing more emphasis on ROK interdependence with its trade partners worldwide and trying to project a better state image throughout the international system. This was an interesting development from Japan's vantage point because of the many parallels this approach had to Japan's concept of comprehensive security, which was predicated on building harmonious ties that would prevent tensions which could lead to conflict. While South Korea was not explicit about how it developed this concept, it is likely that Japan's revised security policy was another role model for the ROK.

Had the end of the Cold War and dissolution of the Soviet Union brought North Korea to its senses, the odds are Japan would have joined with South Korea and other countries in rescuing it from any sort of collapse scenario. North Korea's decision to pursue a harder line, more autarkic form of nuclear-based deterrence clearly changed all that. This decision was important for many observers, but it was particularly sensitive in Japan—a country whose pacifist security inhibitions are predicated on memories of being the only country in the world to have been on the receiving end of an atomic bomb attack. As the United States took the lead in applying nonproliferation criteria to North Korea's nuclear program, Japan enthusiastically rallied around the cause. Initially Japan did so in a rather circumspect manner by trying to engage North Korea in a dialogue to convince it to change course and by exploring incentives that could induce the DPRK to abandon its reckless brinkmanship policies. Japan became an active participant in the Korean Peninsula Energy Development Organization (KEDO), and encouraged United Nations economic development programs that might persuade Pyongyang to change its policies. That relatively low-key approach halted after North Korea fired a Taepo-dong missile over Japan into the Pacific Ocean in August 1998. That act reinvigorated a sporadic debate within Japan about how far it should go in becoming a full-fledged military power. As much as that watershed event is crucial to Japan's national security policy, with many implications for all its neighbors and all major powers, it was particularly acute for the two Koreas since many in both Koreas had feared that Japan would someday regain the means to take further military action against the Korean nation. The fact that a North Korean act had spurred the Japanese to reconsider whether they want to develop the military means of what the Japanese have come to refer to as a "normal country" is a cause of genuine concern for both Koreas. On the other hand, and somewhat mitigating that Korean anxiety, Japan has also used North Korea's provocations as a rationale to become more supportive of a budding inter-Korean peace process that has the potential to devise a solution to the problems provoked by North Korea's actions.[5]

In the years since that missile launch, Japan has displayed its readiness to play a larger military role worldwide in cooperation with both the United Nations and the United States, focusing on peace-keeping and peace-building endeavors. More salient for present purposes, Japan also has had several military confrontations with North Korean vessels. Japan clearly has sent a message to North Korea that it will not respond passively. Although Japan also has been an active member of the United States-ROK-Japan Trilateral Coordination and Oversight Group (TCOG) intended to bring the United States and its two Northeast Asian allies into greater harmony collectively on the nuclear issue, it has had limited success. Japan also is a member of the ongoing Six-Party Talks, intended to induce North Korea to become more accommodating. Japan's efforts on the military and diplomatic portions of its policy spectrum have sent an unintentionally mixed signal.

That situation became more intense in the post-9/11 atmosphere of U.S. policy toward the two Koreas. The Bush administration's hard-line policies, embodied in the Bush Doctrine and its concept of military preemption, and President Bush's animosity toward Kim Jong-il, whom he declared loathsome, clearly have caused skepticism among South Korea's progressive leaders in the Kim Dae-jung and Roh Moo-hyun administrations. While many in the Japanese public may share that skepticism about U.S. policies, the conservative government under the Koizumi administration that held office at the same time as Roh and Bush, clearly was empathetic toward a more hard-line approach to North Korea, critical of Roh, and uneasy about the prospects of China gaining more clout in guiding the inter-Korean efforts to resolve the tensions created by the DPRK's nuclear option. Despite two efforts by Koizumi to generate a Japan-DPRK bilateral dialogue supportive of the broader peace process, via Koizumi–Kim Jong-il summits in Pyongyang (September 2002 and May 2004), Japan under Koizumi has experienced a strong wave of anti–North Korean sentiments, provoked by revelations of DPRK kidnappings of Japanese. In this atmosphere in 2003–2004, Japan launched spy satellites aimed at North Korea, asserted Japan's right to use a preemptive strike doctrine against a potential threat, and joined the United States in a de facto blockade against North Korea intended to induce change. Although Japan has not gone as far in a hard-liner direction as the United States has, the U.S.-Japanese approaches to North Korea are much closer to each other than either the United States or Japan is to South Korea's peaceful engagement approach. Whether this will help North Korea and/or the PRC in their relations with South Korea remains to be seen, but unless there is a major change in Japanese-U.S. policies toward Korea, these differences raise many questions about the Korean peninsula's place in the international system.

KOREA AND OTHER COUNTRIES

Lest the concluding comments on Japan's role vis-à-vis Korea end this chapter on a pessimistic note, it is important to include some observations on other sectors of the international community's relations with the Korean peninsula. Two predictable factors stand out: South Korea's economic appeal and North Korea's nuclear recklessness.

Given South Korea's economic stature, achieved over the second half of the twentieth century, and the emphasis that the ROK has put upon regional and global interdependence, it is no surprise that South Korea is held in high esteem by many countries that either see it as a role model for developing countries or acknowledge the ROK's major importance as a trading partner for a number of countries in Europe, the Middle East, Latin America, South and Southeast Asia, and Australasia-Oceania. When one considers that during the Korean War era virtually no one entertained the thought that South Korea was or would become an economic dynamo warranting widespread interest, this is a truly remarkable achievement. Just as it is important to note, within the context of the ROK's foreign policy, the importance of an evolving "pie chart" metaphor which illustrates the changing ratio of various countries' importance to South Korea, many other countries' version of such pie charts since the 1960s would show a larger and larger slice represented by the ROK.

For a number of these countries that value their economic relationship with South Korea, the actions taken by North Korea in pursuit of its nuclear option poses a dual threat. Not only is it inherently destabilizing, it endangers all those countries' relationships with the other Korea and with the prospect that South Koreans often hold out for global consideration, namely a future unified Korea that will amount to a larger version of what the ROK is today. Such a prospective united Korea would be an even more attractive trading partner for all those countries currently enjoying a positive relationship with South Korea.

As important as that hypothetical factor is for other countries that have a stake in the Korean peninsula, all those countries in the Asian region that would experience the repercussions of any war resulting from a total failure of the inter-Korean peace process are especially attuned to fostering means to persuade North Korea and its adversaries to prevent such a war. As emphasized by the Southeast Asian states that constitute the Association of South East Asian Nations (ASEAN), there are multiple reasons for them to encourage the two Koreas and the four major powers to find a solution. Were a war to break out over North Korea's nuclear posturing, the damage done in Korea would undoubtedly be profoundly worth avoiding. While the damage might well extend offshore, most likely to Japan, where U.S. forces committed to Korean security probably would be targeted, North Korea also would likely target Japan—per se—if it overtly supported any U.S. military actions against North Korea. As serious as all that is for the ASEAN countries, another daunting prospect that could directly affect their well being is the chance that the United States and China might clash over how to handle such a crisis. Japan's possible role in any such trans-Pacific development also would be of concern. Because of such issues, and because of the inherent difficulties in creating an organized Northeast Asian counterpart to ASEAN, its members have expanded its purview via the ASEAN Regional Forum (ARF) to encourage a broader dialogue on nonproliferation issues than can, inter alia, help resolve the North Korean nuclear crisis.

On a far broader scale, the same process is at work through various organizations within the United Nations. Such groups are useful for a variety of countries to use as global institutions that can act as facilitators for confidence-building among North Korean leaders. This may yet induce them to accept the concessions necessary for avoiding the disaster that may lie before the DPRK if it does not make innovative changes and reforms. All such UN-linked international efforts, as well as those of the four powers and ASEAN assessed above, help to set the stage for Korea's unification prospects evaluated in the final two chapters.

CHAPTER 8

Reuniting the Korean Nation

As the title of this volume, *Korea, the Divided Nation*, intentionally suggests, and as the contextual analysis provided in the first four chapters pointedly confirms, the division of the Korean nation into two states in the 1940s was a disservice to the Korean people. It should never have happened. As important, it should be resolved through Korean reunification as rapidly as possible. This chapter shall examine two broad facets of the problems associated with recreating a single Korean nation-state: (1) what sorts of efforts have been and are being made to foster inter-Korean tension reduction and reconciliation, and (2) what are the possibilities for creating a united Korean nation-state in the foreseeable future? Following upon these assessments, the final chapter in this volume will evaluate the prognosis for a united Korea in the international system.

INTER-KOREAN TENSION REDUCTION

In order to understand how Koreans have tried to come to grips with reducing the tensions that plagued a divided Korea since the late 1940s, it is crucial to grasp the perspectives they bring to bear on the problem, rather than those which Westerners assume. Clearly the Koreans focus on the most obvious aspects of the problem, such as their territorial separation, the ideological gap that has been inculcated among them by outsiders, the geopolitical pressures exerted by regional and global players, and the economic, political, and military frictions that stem from all of these factors. Less clear to non-Korean observers, but equally important as contributing factors are the original cultural and linguistic differences among subgroups within the Korean nation.

To foreigners, a Korean is a Korean. It is usually difficult for most foreigners to detect regional identities among them. However, these differences do exist and can become significant in terms of treatment of one's fellow Koreans. For example, within South Korea it is all too common for people in Seoul or the southeastern Kyongsan provinces to display condescension toward the regional accent and historical heritage of people from the southwestern Cholla provinces. This regionalism held back the economic development of those provinces for a while and accentuated the controversy surrounding the Kwangju uprising in 1980. There are other regional frictions within both South and North Korea and, more important for present purposes, between southern and northern Koreans of various sorts that have nothing directly to do with the fact that they live in the ROK or the DPRK. Such frictions are derived from their heritages and the memories passed down through many generations that feed stereotypes and biases. Many northerners see themselves as more rugged and resilient that effete southerners, whereas comparable southerners see themselves as more civilized and sophisticated compared to northern country bumpkins. Making such matters worse for contemporary Koreans on both ends of the peninsula are the ways half a century of rigid division have added ideological layers to such stereotypes, the ways each Korea's socioeconomic development has exposed its people to radically different ways of life, and the ways each Korea's population has been exposed to different foreign cultures and languages that have found their way into each Korea's popular culture. These influences are sufficiently strong that some of the people who have participated in emotional North-South reunions with family members they have not seen for decades report they have had difficulty in communicating with each other because of the ways their separate vocabularies have evolved.

It is clear that the governments of both North and South Korea can and should do more to prepare each one's share of the Korean nation for the nuanced problems of cultural reconciliation. Since both Koreas have to cope with internal regional frictions, each can use the efforts made to minimize those domestic societal divisions as a paradigm for pan-national efforts to develop an appreciation for cultural cohesion. The more the two Koreas engage in such confidence-building cultural activities, the better prepared they will be for engaging in the more visible political, economic, and strategic dialogues that are necessary for Korean reunification.

Against that backdrop a summary of the past efforts of Koreans on both sides to reduce bilateral tensions, build mutual confidence, and set the stage for Korean reconciliation leading to reunification can be offered. In the very early post–World War II years, prior to the creation of the ROK and the DPRK, a plausible case can be made that the sporadic contacts would-be leaders in both portions of occupied Korea had with each other and their ability to discuss a common future prior to the creation of a demarcation border between two states might have been sufficient to generate movement toward one Korean state had the U.S.-USSR tensions of the escalating Cold War not derailed their efforts. After the U.S.- and Soviet-backed rival Korean states came into existence, however, the leaders of each Korea had new incentives to push for each one's interpretation of what could have been a shared vision of a common future. As the Cold War environment provided each Korea with political, financial, and strategic reasons to think its version of the future was superior to the alternative offered by the other side, the gap that divided them grew far beyond the line on the map and everything it symbolized. Whatever chance there was that the two Koreas could have overcome that growing gap was severely undermined by the Korean War's impact on both halves of Korea and each one's network with its international supporters. In short, for a couple of decades after the Korean War, there was little prospect that the two Koreas might reach peaceful coexistence, much less genuine progress toward reunification.

Despite all that, for the leaders of both Koreas, the concept of unification took on an almost mythological aura, making it a politically sacrosanct touchstone imbued with profound meaning. These leaders frequently cited their commitment to the goal of unification, spelled out specific proposals that seemed well intended from the perspective of one of the two Koreas but were guaranteed to be rejected by the other Korea because of its rival interests. There were numerous efforts of that sort which warrant scholarly attention,[1] and some of them from the ROK in their day appeared to be taken seriously—such as a proposal by Park Chung-hee in November 1961 for UN support for unification, periodic Park proposals for expanded dialogues that enjoyed limited success in 1972 via the creation of a North-South Coordinating Committee, and comparable updates under Chun Doo-hwan. Equivalent efforts by the DPRK—such as Kim Il-sung's periodic proposals from 1957 until his death in 1994 for mutual force cuts, removing all foreign forces, various exchange programs, and from 1960 until 1994 for discussing Korean confederation—were acknowledged, but deemed to be far less credible. Despite the attention such proposals received when they were raised, attention which can be ascribed to the desire of the Korean public for such goals to be pursued even if in vain, those proposals deserve to be categorized largely as gestures and rhetoric. They were meant to provide succor to all those Koreans who wanted efforts to be made.

Although backers of such proposals in both Koreas insist they were, and are, totally sincere in pressing for a unitary, federalized, or confederalized state, and they do not appreciate any criticism to the contrary, there is ample reason to be profoundly skeptical about claims of sincerity.[2] From the stalemate of the Korean War until the end of the Cold War, supposedly serious efforts by both Koreas to create the means to reduce tension, build confidence, and create peace have regularly and consciously operated in what American legislators often refer to as a "free vote" environment. That phrase means that it is totally safe to advocate a policy that one does not actually desire in circumstances where there is no chance of that policy being achieved and put into operation because of its opponents' strength. The means to assure that a free vote will remain "free" is to—borrowing a phrase from U.S. legislators—be certain there is a "poison pill" of unacceptable specifics embedded in the proposed policy that will be absolutely intolerable to those on the receiving end of the proposal. Clearly these free vote and poison pill aspects of proposals on inter-Korean reconciliation have been deftly worded so that their negative qualities are not at all obvious, but appear to be consistent with a sincere proposal for their common good.

The reasons both Koreas used such means stem from the vested interests of the leadership elite of each Korea in their respective system and each one's inability to conceive of ways they could merge without significant loss of power and—in Confucian terms—societal face. Each side had reason to hope and expect that its backers would prevail in the larger global milieu. That, coupled with the authoritarian political culture that was influential in South Korea throughout the Cold War years and has been in total control of the DPRK since its inception, created conditions conducive to gestures, rhetoric, and manipulation that could not be readily contested by potential critics within either Korea. In this setting the inter-Korean blame game persisted amid scattered semi-realistic efforts that stood virtually no chance of succeeding but were sufficient to mollify the underlying mass aspirations for eventual progress. As time passed the North-South rift persisted and, as DPRK internal conditions worsened, the gap between the two Koreas that would have to be bridged grew far more severe and arguably ominous. Despite occasional claims to the contrary, no genuine progress on reunification was being achieved and the prospects were growing dimmer.

That bleak milieu was altered dramatically by a series of developments roughly concurrent with, and loosely linked to, the end of the Cold War. The dissolution of the Soviet Union and end of the U.S.-USSR Cold War injected fundamental changes into the two Koreas' unification context. Without the superpower communist versus anticommunist dynamic as a framework for the two Koreas to shape their reconciliation debate, a major prop was eliminated. Most obviously North Korea no longer had the Soviet Union as one of its supporters, thereby losing part of its leverage, and making it far more subject to PRC pressures. The DPRK also knew its U.S. adversary no longer had its major adversary in the world and the region, making U.S. motivations for staying strategically committed in Northeast Asia far more subject to debate. This injected new uncertainties into DPRK-ROK relations. In that vein South Korea had to ponder how the DPRK would respond to these changes. Seoul also had to consider how the ROK's alliance relationship with the United States might be affected over the long term by the lack of a regionalized Soviet threat to the United States, which led Americans to debate the advantages of a peace dividend and whether it would be useful for South Korea to encourage the United States to focus more on North Korea in it own right.

As these post–Cold War issues were being contemplated, the related issue of German unification created another new context for both Koreas. For the DPRK the concessions by East Germany, when coupled with Gorbachev's changes in the devolving Soviet Union, sent ominous signals. Although the ROK had more reasons to be a joyful observer of German and Soviet changes, the combination of North Korean anxieties and profound South Korean unease about whether the ROK had neglected to prepare itself sufficiently for success was daunting. Despite South Korea's economic stature, ties to advanced countries worldwide, and significant efforts to learn from West Germany's *Ostpolitik* model via the ROK's *Nordpolitik* policy early in the Roh Tae-woo administration, Seoul was clearly shaken by how fast matters had evolved in Germany and Russia and experienced transparent doubts about the ROK's ability to cope with the challenges that might be nearer over the horizon than South Korean conventional wisdom had presumed.

Beyond those two issues emerging outside the confines of the Korean peninsula, the milieu affecting Korean unification prospects was seriously changed by developments within both Koreas. Undoubtedly the most noticed factor involved the DPRK's pursuit of a nuclear option via reckless brinkmanship, which adversely influenced the prospects for a peaceful outcome on the peninsula, and the ways North Korea's post–Cold War socioeconomic deterioration raised the likelihood of its total collapse. These two facets of post–Cold War North Korea can be perceived from two basic dimensions. The prevailing estimate of what they represent in North Korea focuses on the danger they pose in terms of the DPRK becoming an unstable power whose economy could erode in ways that will increase the chances of the DPRK selling its nuclear know-how to other rogue states or to terrorist groups. Another way of evaluating these two factors is that North Korea's focus on its nuclear brinkmanship, given the uncertainties about what nuclear assets the DPRK actually possesses, may well be the basis for enhanced psychological deterrence that plays on other countries' fears in ways that may make them amenable to engaging in negotiations, which Pyongyang can use to acquire the wherewithal to prevent its economy from suffering a collapse.

Far less noticed on a worldwide basis was the way South Korea's post–Cold War expansion of authentic democratic processes altered the ability of both Koreas to continue to engage in a dialogue in which their rhetoric is excessive, their sincerity is questionable, and their results are minimal. As South Korean political progressives gained traction during the Kim Dae-jung and Roh Moo-hyun administrations, they creatively questioned why the results of past reconciliation dialogue efforts had been so slim in prior administrations. Equally important these progressive support groups pressed for more candor regarding how ROK and DPRK concepts of a merger could be made mutually acceptable. This effectively opened the South Korean intellectual marketplace more than it had been previously to listening to North Korean notions of what might be desirable. As time passed these trends were intensified by the demographic generational shift occurring in Korea, which in South Korea yielded a far more liberal cohort of younger voters, who tipped the balance in favor of President Roh's election. These trends also contributed to popular opinion in South Korea becoming far more skeptical of the influences the United States and Japan had on ROK flexibility in negotiating with the DPRK.

The net result of this changed milieu became evident in the bold initiative launched by Kim Dae-jung when he assumed the presidency in early 1998, in the form of his Sunshine Policy.[3] The name was derived from *Aesop's Fables*, which led to some skepticism about its seriousness, but it arguably has been South Korea's most profound effort to engage North Korea in meaningful discussions. Partly because of North Korea's desires to maximize its bargaining position with the Clinton administration over nuclear-related issues, make better use of what KEDO could do for the DPRK, and use improved ROK-DPRK dialogue processes to enhance North Korea's access to other multilateral venues, Pyongyang responded to Seoul's overtures to a degree not experienced previously. In short, the Sunshine Policy succeeded in getting representatives from both Koreas to sit around a series of tables to discuss a great variety of issues in ways that had the potential to become truly meaningful. Kim Dae-jung's June 2000 summit with Kim Jong-il in Pyongyang, the two Koreas' agreement to have their teams at the September 2000 Sydney Olympics march under a joint flag (white with a blue Korean peninsula) at the opening ceremony, and President Kim's receiving the Nobel Peace Prize for his efforts, became highly visible examples of the new milieu. As many publications from the ROK Ministry of Unification, Office of the North-South Dialogue, attest, there is ample documentation of the diversity of contacts since the Sunshine Policy took effect. Even though U.S. support for that policy diminished after the Clinton-Bush transition, including reported efforts to get DJ to drop the "Sunshine" label, Seoul resisted criticism that its engagement campaign amounted to appeasement, involved de facto bribery, and persisted in trying to cultivate an expanded dialogue with Pyongyang.

The United States' harder line approach toward North Korea under President Bush created problems for Seoul in terms of North Korea's efforts to take advantage of an opportunity to drive a wedge deeper within the United States-ROK alliance and DJ's need to cope with domestic conservatives who sought to take political advantage by siding with Bush. This entire situation was jolted by the 9/11 terrorist attacks on the United States that caused Washington to toughen its posture toward all threats, pointedly including rogue states such as North Korea, which got lumped together with Iraq and Iran as the "axis of evil" by President Bush in his 2002 State of the Union Address. Although the great majority of South Koreans and the DPRK, in an official statement, expressed sympathy for what had happened to the United States on 9/11, the ways the Bush administration expanded its reaction to include a harder line stance on North Korea and lessened support for DJ's inter-Korean dialogue initiatives provoked a wave of anti-Bush sentiment throughout the peninsula.

That atmosphere clearly contributed to the election of President Roh Moo-hyun, whose supporters favored President Kim's engagement stance regarding North Korea and opposed the harder line positions of the Bush administration. After Roh was in office, some conservatives in South Korea viewed Roh as the anti-Bush symbol and deemed some of Roh's appointees as pro-Pyongyang. Roh's very liberal presidential campaign statements that urged greater ROK resistance to groveling before the United States and suggested South Korea might be ready to be a mediator between the United States and the DPRK suggested the tone of his administration. President Roh persisted in using a modified form of the Sunshine Policy, now relabeled the "Policy for Peace and Prosperity," in order to enhance its marketability. The Roh administration, despite its problems with Washington over North Korea and the domestic political turmoil Roh had to confront, managed to remain committed to an expanded inter-Korean dialogue process. As of early 2005 significant progress in terms of the first ever ROK-DPRK military-to-military negotiations, agreements to open roads and railways for inter-Korean commerce, agreements on maritime tension reduction, and agreements on stopping DMZ propaganda had been arranged. These reinforced the ways the ROK was using the Six-Party Talks (United States, PRC, Japan, Russia, and the two Koreas) on the nuclear topic hosted by Beijing to reinforce South Korea's engagement efforts with North Korea. In contrast to earlier examples of poison pill–laden proposals calculated to allow Seoul a free vote, Kim Dae-jung and—especially—Roh Moo-hyun appear to have jettisoned such tactics in favor of a negotiating strategy infused with genuine sincerity. Time will tell whether these efforts will yield lasting successful results in terms of getting North Korea on board in ways that are truly meaningful.

REUNIFICATION SCENARIOS

There is a virtually infinite spectrum of scenarios for reuniting the two Koreas in terms of the time frame involved, the relative roles of each Korea, the prospective roles of external players, and the built-in problems that any of these categories would have to incorporate. Many analysts in both Koreas and Korea-watchers in other countries have engaged in much speculation and advocacy about the pros and cons of different variables. This includes a cross-section of U.S. analysts without ethnic ties to Korea as well as many Korean American analysts. In short, there is no shortage of perspectives on this issue.

Perhaps the best way to explain these options is to start with the basic ingredients that any solution shall have to incorporate. Korean writers on this topic often seem to be too close to the sensitive issues at stake, in terms of siding with one Korea over the other, to be truly impartial about getting a handle on the data. There are non-Korean analysts who have thoroughly addressed this data with reasonable impartiality.[4] Briefly outlined, the two Koreas' population base is decidedly unequal in terms of South Korea being roughly double the size of North Korea. Plus, South Korea's population tends to be better educated, wealthier, healthier, more worldly in their experiences, and more capable of adjusting to changes. On the face of it, South Korea would seem to have many advantages. It does, but North Korea also has attributes that give it bargaining leverage. These include the North's reputation for a better natural resource base in terms of mineral deposits and hydroelectric power. Whether that reputation is as deserved today as it was during the Japanese colonial era is very debatable, but it could be fully warranted and is often highly esteemed in South Korean circles, who seem to draw upon the image of the past. The DPRK also possesses a significantly larger military compared to the ROK, between 1 and 1.2 million persons versus about 700,000. In that vein, the North's militaristic regimentation can be seen as an advantage. Thus, despite North Korea's relative disadvantages, it clearly has bargaining leverage in any prospective unification process.

As interesting as all such comparisons are, they are mainly useful in terms of the impact they are likely to have on the resulting single Korean nation-state that will blend the attributes of both Koreas and how smoothly that blend can function in the real world. That issue is addressed in the concluding chapter. They are secondarily useful in terms of the ways they might influence each Korea to see the other both as a bargainer and as a potential partner in one Korea. Without being cavalier about these built-in problems, it is more useful for present purposes to move on to the larger issues at stake.

Foremost in that regard is the prospective time frame for Korean reconciliation and reunification. If one were to believe the rhetoric of past advocates of unification in both Koreas, one would have to assume they wanted in instantly, preferably yesterday, but pragmatically the sooner the better. While such advocates may have been emotionally sincere, in practice it was a classic free vote expression of a policy goal because they not only knew it would not happen, but it could not happen, nor was it truly desirable because of the inherent complications. As post–Cold War inter-Korean realism took root in both Koreas, it swiftly became evident that gradualist incremental scenarios for a time frame were far more practical and desirable.

When South Koreans examined the costs of German unification, compared the ROK's ability to do for North Korea what West Germany did for East Germany, and examined the impact of East Germany upon united Germany's status in Europe, many in South Korea were shaken. ROK estimates of what it might cost South Korea to follow the West German model ran to more than $2 trillion. That daunting figure was made still more profound by the 1997–1998 economic crisis and by growing concerns about the North Korean economy's continuing decline. While North Korea would not bear any of the financial burdens of being rescued, it clearly rejected the notion that it was prepared to be absorbed by its rival the way East Germany was.

As a consequence of those shared concerns, Seoul's use of the Sunshine Policy/Policy of Peace and Prosperity agenda laid out a longer term vision that could go on for several decades. During that period South Korea, and any of its backers willing to help in the process, would negotiate ways to assist North Korea in closing the socioeconomic gap between the DPRK and the ROK in a manner that would ease the way to a harmonious embrace of common interests en route to reconciliation and reunification. The appeal of this scenario is clear in that it can avoid some of the nastier scenarios that Korea analysts speculate about. Three stand out. One deals with the all-too-real possibility of an abject economic collapse of North Korea. This would force South Korea to absorb a ruined system, cope with impoverished people, and deal with the consequences in a weak united Korea. Another deals with how North Korea might overreact to the possibility of its collapse or of an outside power trying to compel changes in the DPRK. This could lead to a last-gasp war launched by the DPRK, designed to inflict its solution on the peninsula by force of arms even at the risk of taking all of Korea down with it in defeat. That could be a disastrous way to unify Korea. The third entails a U.S.-led military effort at "regime change" in Pyongyang that would rapidly topple the regime but leave South Korea at the center of picking up the pieces as it assembled a unified Korean state.

While longer term scenarios may well be desirable for both Koreas, one can also visualize shorter term scenarios that could make sense. Several examples are worth noting. Given Kim Jong-il's obvious desire to have an inter-Korean solution be achieved while he is charge of the DPRK's role in creating that solution, an accelerated form of Seoul's gradualism—between five to fifteen years—could make considerable sense for both Koreas. On another front, one might visualize the year 2010 as a target date for reunification because it is the 100th anniversary of Japan's takeover in Korea, which began the process that led to Korea's postwar division. Both Koreas have reasons to want to resolve their national division prior to that centennial date. The gradualist process also could be speeded up if the United States and/or other countries such as China, Japan, Russia, and the European Union were to help South Korea do for all of Korea what West Germany did for Germany.[5] That solution at an accelerated pace could produce the same results anticipated via the prolonged gradualist vision, but without having to put it off for so long that it could complicate the cultural imbalances between the two Koreas.

Whether the negotiations process turns out to be prolonged or accelerated, the parameters of the negotiations will matter greatly for how Koreans dwelling in a future united Korea, and all other countries dealing with a united Korea, shall perceive the identity of that state. A strong argument can be made that Koreans in both Koreas will be better served if their leaders are able to truly take the lead in the quest for Korean reconciliation and reunification without the assistance or intervention of any external power. It would be best if the theories behind the negotiations process, the motivations behind the political, economic, and strategic agendas, and the locale for hosting the sequence of meetings leading to Korea's resolution of its divided nation problems can all be dealt with by Koreans in Korea. Non-Koreans should support Koreans in pursuing that goal if they can arrange it for themselves, should avoid trying to influence their pursuit of that goal, and should welcome whatever results the Koreans may devise—even if it is not fully in accord with what might be on the other countries' wish list for how a united Korea should configure itself. Having put this viewpoint on the record, it must be acknowledged that the chances of the two Koreas—given their differences, legacy of enmity, and ties to a range of external players—being able to devise a resolution totally on their own are extraordinarily slim. It is not impossible, but is likely to be very close to impossible.

Therefore, on the assumption that the two Koreas will require one or more outside players to help them get their act together en route to reunification, it is worthwhile surveying these scenarios too. It is very likely that the prime candidates for playing such a role are already engaged in Korean affairs bilaterally and through the Six-Party Talks. Two of them, Russia and Japan, with all due respect, must be relegated to the less-than-likely category. Both possess serious expertise on Korean affairs that may well be called upon by either or both Koreas for advice. Both also possess major reasons, as neighbors and in light of their well-known national interests in Korean stability and prosperity, to want to help when and where they can. That, too, may well be welcomed by either or both Koreas. However, and it is a huge "however," both Japan and Russia possess liabilities in terms of their historical legacies, institutional vulnerabilities, and occasional cultural frictions that make them doubtful as facilitators or catalysts in the inter-Korean peace process. Neither can be counted out in that regard—although Japan comes close—but their prospects are far dimmer than the other two.

Clearly the United States and China are much better positioned to play such a role in terms of their capabilities, regional interests, global interests, expertise on the issues involved, and—perhaps most important—their moral obligations to do the right thing for Korea in light of their past relations. A strong case can be made on behalf of either major power. The United States has major reasons to see its way through to what Selig Harrison insightfully labeled its "endgame" in Korea.[6] Even some U.S. conservatives who may well disagree with his progressive analysis should acknowledge the logic of helping the Koreans wrap up a divided nation's problems, which the United States participated in instigating. Beyond that, the United

States' economic, military, and diplomatic power and expertise are major assets that can help the two Koreas tremendously, if Washington is prepared to help. Interestingly many of the same things can be said about China's potential role as a helper for the two Koreas. The major exception is with regard to the "endgame" metaphor because for China—as Korea's largest neighbor and given Korea's past role in a Sinocentric regional system—that concept does not apply.

That difference between these two potential facilitators or catalysts is very significant in terms of U.S.-PRC relations in the entire Asia-Pacific region where many Americans perceive China as a rising power and where many Chinese (and others) consider the United States to be a global and regional hegemon that is intent upon blocking any rivals from challenging U.S. power. In those terms each of these major powers' potential roles in helping in the Korean peace process could lead to a united Korea being geopolitically indebted to either China or the United States. That could have serious implications for how each power sees its national interests vis-à-vis the Korean peninsula in the Northeast Asian context. China has already been setting the stage for greater Korean reliance on the PRC's economy, its regional leadership aspirations, and—to a lesser extent—its geopolitical vision. Partly because the United States is wary of where that may lead, the United States seems to want to remain the key partner for South Korea and assumes this will lead to a transition someday into a comparable role for a united Korea. However, the United States has not been handling its ROK ally very well in the context of the ROK-DPRK peace process linkages to North Korean nuclear brinkmanship or in terms of instilling confidence among South Koreans about U.S. leadership of the post-9/11 world.

Because of these uncertainties, it is plausible that either the United States or China could end up playing the major external role in the inter-Korean reconciliation and reunification process. Given the uncertainties noted, both China and the United States should consider yet another of the scenarios the two Koreas confront, namely working in tandem with a regional multilateral team of facilitators. The Six-Party Talks package may well be a precedent for this. So, too, might some of the ASEAN countries—given their ARF involvement—become part of a group helping the two Koreas. It is also conceivable that the European Union might play a role. As plausible as all of these options might be, and as attractive as they could be to both Koreas, it is also conceivable that the United States and China might work together as a team that could do many things to help the two Koreas become one nation-state, but do so in a manner that does not aggravate U.S.-PRC relations or inject new post-unification strains surrounding Korea, which could result from only one of the big powers playing such a helpful role.

To wrap up these options, it is worthwhile acknowledging a somewhat utopian scenario, namely the prospects for the United Nations playing a decisive role in helping the two Koreas get their national act together. In one sense this might be perfect because it could be the basis for such a diffuse form of multilateral assistance that no single power would get too much credit or too much blame for how things turn out. In that respect, even if many countries lend a hand via the United Nations, the two Koreas could legitimately claim that the core resolutions were the result of Korean decisions and Korean actions. Also, given the UN role in both Koreas since the UN-backed election created the ROK during the Korean War, and since the Korean War, there certainly is a plausible case to be made to try to use it to help the Korean reconciliation and reunification process. As much as some variation of this scenario may appeal to many Koreans and to many others throughout the world, it must be acknowledged that the UN track record in such affairs leaves much to be desired. Therefore, the prospects for this scenario are not as good as some of those already evaluated.

Against the backdrop of the prospective scenarios for Korean unification outlined here, and bearing in mind all of the factors explained in chapter 7 about the perspectives of the four major powers with an established stake in Korean affairs, it is worthwhile concluding this chapter with what amounts to a prescriptive policy postscript. Clearly such policy advocacy can be done from the vantage point of any of the four powers, either of the two Koreas, or from a generic Korean perspective. All such policy advocacy should be encouraged as part of a healthy debate over how to rectify the problems stemming from Korea being a divided nation for so many years.

Every effort was made in preparing this volume to present a balanced view of the circumstances in both Koreas, between the two

Koreas, and surrounding them internationally. Nonetheless, it is safe to assume that many readers—whether or not they perused the author's biographical note—will have detected an inclination toward American interests in Korea. That should be expected from virtually any American analyst of Korean affairs, especially in a volume intended as background reading for an American audience that wants to know more about Korea. The same would be true of a Russian, Japanese, or Chinese analyst of Korean affairs writing for an audience in any of those countries. Just as any such author would be well advised to draw conclusions about what Moscow, Tokyo, or Beijing should do about the problems represented by a divided Korean nation, so too is it worthwhile to offer normative advice on how the United States can best improve its policy toward Korea. This is especially crucial given the United States' role in Korea's division, Korea's open-ended partition, and Korea's environment for reconciliation and reunification.

As explained in several contexts above, the United States deserves credit for becoming more sophisticated over the years about Korean affairs, remaining committed to helping Korea, and exploring some innovative options. Whether U.S. efforts, perhaps in conjunction with the two Koreas or with another major power—notably China—have been sufficient is legitimately debatable. It is clear that there is a broad spectrum of views within the U.S. foreign policy and Korea-specialist communities. That kind of debate has evolved in productive ways. As healthy as it is for U.S. society, and as productive as it could be, the ways the debate are carried out leave something to be desired. All too often advocates and critics of various positions expound their views in ways that do not involve face-to-face confrontations in settings where a clash of normative pros and cons would be extremely useful to U.S. policy makers to hear and watch.

Although the scope of this analysis has been intentionally diverse, the prescriptive postscript offered in conclusion is equally intentionally specific. If the United States is ever to reach a national consensus about how to improve U.S. policy toward ending Korea's division through unification, the U.S. bureaucracy needs to develop the appropriate infrastructure to be exposed to the healthy debate over policy options and work with counterparts in both Koreas and other countries to generate a meaningful dialogue. The best way to do this would be for the U.S. government to work with American academic centers and think tanks with expertise on Korean studies to create a U.S. center or institute for Korean unification affairs that would amount to an institutional counterpart to the organizations that exist in South Korea and North Korea. Such an organization might be part of the U.S. government or it might be sanctioned by the U.S. government but established in a nongovernmental setting. This center/institute could regularly host conferences and workshops, publish analyses, and sponsor visiting Korean specialists in inter-Korean affairs—from both North Korea and South Korea—to participate in a broad range of activities. Creating such an organization and integrating its activities into a framework providing information to U.S. policy makers and their working-level advisors would be a very positive step.

Obviously accepting and implementing this recommendation would not guarantee success for U.S. policy toward a divided Korean nation. However, it would greatly improve the prospects for U.S. success by improving the American policy debate format, accelerating the U.S.-Korean dialogue process, and demonstrating U.S. sincerity in seeking a practical consensus toward a truly viable policy. If it does not work, the United States will earn credit for trying more than it now does. If it does help the process of improving U.S. policy toward reuniting Korea, using some variation of the scenarios outlined here, then the eventual results in a united Korea will be better known to the American people and their leaders well in advance—permitting the United States to prepare for a productive and harmonious relationship with a united Korea.

CHAPTER 9

Conclusion: United Korea's Prospects

Precisely what a United Korea sovereign state would look like and how it would behave internationally is impossible to predict, but—with or without a crystal ball—one can frame the likely parameters of that prospective state, based on the odds for and against elements contained in the scenarios surveyed in the previous chapter.

Two possible ways for a United Korea to swiftly become a version of the ROK or the DPRK would be as the result of either: (1) one Korea conquering the other Korea, or (2) one Korea collapsing or imploding and then being abjectly absorbed by the other Korea. In the first case, the chances of such a war occurring are slim, and few—if any—on either side seem to want a war of that magnitude. As important, even if such a war were to occur and yield either the ROK or the DPRK as the survivor in charge of the peninsula, it is virtually certain that the damage inflicted on both Koreas by the war would guarantee that the resulting United Korea could not be an expanded version of either the ROK or the DPRK. It would be a severely traumatized and diminished version of one or the other. The second category is more plausible in light of North Korea's decrepit infrastructure, economic ineptitude, famine-induced health problems, and dictatorial inflexibility, all of which make it a prime candidate for regime failure. However, that bleak aura has surrounded the DPRK for many years and it has managed to survive and function. Equally important, these all-too-real prospects of collapse constitute a serious incentive for the leaders in Pyongyang to negotiate their way out of being coercively absorbed by the ROK in the process of becoming one Korea.

As powerful as these counterarguments are as reasons why the previous two outcomes are unlikely, it remains possible that a peaceful negotiating process between North and South Korea yielding a United Korea could spawn a state that would be a large version of one of today's two Koreas. If representatives of the two Koreas carry out rational negotiations, using objective methods, over a long enough period of time to permit North Korea to close the socioeconomic gap between it and South Korea, it is plausible the resulting state and all of its components would amount to a peninsula-wide version of one of the two Koreas. Short of the DPRK successfully catching up with the ROK and surpassing South Korea's socioeconomic prosperity and flexibility, there is no chance that the DPRK would be the model for the future United Korea. To achieve this scenario, the DPRK would have to be bent on transforming itself into a de facto clone of the ROK en route to a merger. Even if North Korea were ever to follow such a course, it is unlikely to enjoy that much success.

The chances of these scenarios yielding a United Korea of that genre do exist, but another variation of the scenario is more promising. Most likely the kinds of societal reforms North Korea would pursue as the negotiating process plays out over time would draw on ROK and PRC role models, blending them with reinterpretations of North Korea's Kimist philosophy. In essence, North Koreans would be most likely to learn from South Korea and China through adaptation to the DPRK's peculiar political culture and strategic culture. This would enable them to North Koreanize these changes sufficiently so that the DPRK's negotiators would be able to cut deals with their ROK counterparts that would effectively blend the ROK socioeconomic and geopolitical models with their adapted equivalents in the DPRK. This would permit North Koreans to do in the future what they refuse to do now, namely look at the ways the former East Germany incrementally learned from West Germany well before permitting itself to join with the other half of Germany. This would become feasible because a DPRK that had truly North Koreanized a reform model rooted in South Korea and China would see itself in a far better position than East Germany had been at that juncture.

If handled prudently, this could be very beneficial for both Koreas en route to becoming one Korea again because it would give both sides the means to credibly claim that the resulting United Korea is legitimately descended from both the DPRK and the ROK. That United Korea would be tilting overwhelmingly toward what the entire world would recognize as a ROK-derived model, but it would have enough DPRK-derived adaptations of the ROK model's economic, political, and strategic reforms to permit all Koreans in a future United Korea to trace their heritage to both Koreas. A key variable in this evolutionary dynamic for the creation of a viable United Korea would be how external players interact with the reconciliation and reunification process as well as the resulting United Korea.

Clearly China and the United States stand out as key prospective facilitators and catalysts for systemic change in Korea. In terms of the North Koreanization variable just assessed, China is far better positioned to play a central role. There is virtually no prospect that North Koreans would want to North Koreanize a U.S.-derived developmental and reform model drawing on the American system which the DPRK has demonized for so long. This does not mean that the United States would be sidelined by that prospective process. After all, even the North Koreans must recognize and acknowledge the influence that U.S. brands of capitalism, democracy, and freedom have had on the ROK and the PRC as well as on other countries from which both have learned—notably Japan. As much as the United States has to face the probability that China would play a significant role in the context of a North Korean adaption paradigm, that would not mean the United States should be passive in other contexts which could both shape a United Korea and condition how it functions after its creation. This would be most true in terms of the United States doing its utmost to assure processes which would produce a United Korea that would incorporate measures assuring it would not possess nuclear weapons.

As noted in the previous chapter there is a plausible scenario in which both China and the United States could influence the peaceful negotiations process, shape the geopolitical environment in which that process would evolve in a way that accelerates its progress, and work together in ways that send signals to the Koreans and the rest of the world that the United States and China's ability to cooperate on a very sensitive Korean issue bodes well for their ability to collaborate on a broad spectrum of other issues central to Asia-Pacific stability and prosperity. So, short of a disastrous disruption of Sino-American relations or a serious setback for China as a rising power in world affairs,[1] it is very much in the national interest of the United States to do its best to work closely with China to help the processes which would yield a United Korea and then move forward to deal with a United Korea as it finds its place in the international system.

The prospective role of a United Korea internationally would be a major consideration for the Koreans who would create a new nation-state as well as for all those countries that would interact with it. It is fitting that this volume, which has examined Korea's experiences as a country that arduously assembled itself as a nation-state from separate ethnic elements over thousands of years, lasted for twelve centuries amidst various challenges, but was torn in two by international forces beyond its ability to control or restrain, should conclude with an overview of how a United Korea might interact internationally in ways that would help it last indefinitely.

Key questions arise on two levels: regionally and globally. A reasonably strong case can be made on behalf of a United Korea wanting to create a niche for itself on both levels as a neutral state.[2] If the leaders of Korea in the future decide that its stability, security, and prosperity could best be provided by following the examples of Switzerland and Sweden, that should be their prerogative. Nonetheless, the realities of Korea having its two proverbial "whales" on either side would cause serious concerns about whether its best option would be as a neutral "shrimp"—even if it were to be a well-armed, self-reliant neutral state analogous to those European examples. It is far more likely that a United Korea would adhere internationally to the legacies it would inherit from its ROK and DPRK predecessors. In other words it would avail itself of international opportunities on local, regional, and global levels to bolster its economic and geopolitical stability.

This spectrum of international opportunities that might be presented to a United Korea is far too complex to present in a succinct format here. International-relations theorists spend their lives theorizing about what might happen, when, and why. In short, nobody can predict such developments for evolving future decades with credible accuracy. Nonetheless, some broad parameters can be suggested. One arena has already been mentioned, namely how the future relationship between the United States and China would shape a United Korea's international setting. Clearly it would matter greatly whether Sino-American interactions are friendly or adversarial. The same would be true for Sino-Japanese relations, with very serious implications for the Korean peninsula either positioned as a crossroads of cooperation or as a vortex of clashing interests. A somewhat similar, though not as profound, case can be made for Sino-Japanese and Russo-Japanese relations with a United Korea on their border. Fortunately for Koreans, the prospects for Russian tensions with either China or Japan does not seem to be on most observers' horizons, so a United Korea could afford to be more optimistic in that context. On balance, however, a United Korea could be expected to pay careful attention to how the four major powers perceive Korean unification, help or hinder the inter-Korean negotiations process, and prepare themselves for either becoming an economic, political, and strategic supporter or ally of a United Korea, or reject such a role entirely. The latter option could be through a policy of abstention, or choosing to oppose a United Korea and any country or group with which it becomes aligned.

If a United Korea were to play its diplomatic and strategic cards deftly, it would strike the right balance within its ties to the four powers for as long as they remain decisive agents of influence in the region. While a solid case can be made for all four remaining influential in Korea's neighborhood, from a Korean perspective two are most certain to remain factors in a United Korea's long-term future, namely the Chinese and Japanese "whales." This regional dynamic would necessitate a United Korea avoiding the shrimp metaphor, maximizing its status in the eyes of these neighbors, and being prepared to work with out-of-area powers in case either China or Japan were to turn against a United Korea. However, a United Korea should avoid using ties with any out-of-area power in a manner that might cause China and/or Japan to perceive such ties as contrary to their national interests. This aspect of a United Korea's foreign ties would make its relations with Russia and the United States more complex.

Compared to a United Korea's ability to be certain that neither China nor Japan will cease to be a significant factor in a United Korea's international relations, Koreans looking to the long-range future can readily visualize Russia either becoming a still weaker state or a state that tilts toward—or perhaps even joins—the European Union, thereby diminishing its prospective role vis-à-vis Korea. Similarly, Koreans can visualize the United States becoming so entangled in other parts of the world that it would scale back or withdraw from Northeast Asia, becoming an advocate of an East or Northeast Asian multilateral security system that would permit the United States to opt out, or—recalling the United States' past policies—that the United States would simply decide to disengage from any number of strategic commitments. In the post-9/11 environment that option could become more plausible, if Americans ever decide to pursue an option enabling the United States to become strategically independent. In short, there are several ways that the United States might completely or partially disengage in order to focus its energies elsewhere in the world, or exclusively on homeland security. Since a United Korea might have to cope with such contingencies vis-à-vis Russia or the United States, its leaders would have an incentive to use preemptive means to try to convince each of these powers to remain interested in Korea so that Korea could have recourse to allying with one or more out-of-area powers in order to cope with any potential problems with either neighboring "whale." As sound as that alternative would be, Korean leaders would have to be wary of untoward Chinese or Japanese reactions to Korean contingency planning.

Beyond these projections of a United Korea's relationships with the same cluster of countries that the ROK and the DPRK have focused on, there are other regional factors it would likely have to address. One is fairly far removed from Korea within Asia as a region, but is virtually a given as a factor that would influence the Asian balance of power in its economic, political, and strategic dimensions, namely, the rise of India as a significant power, with the potential to be on a par with China and Japan. There is little or no risk that India would do anything that would adversely affect a United Korea's prospects as a viable nation-state. Nevertheless, the chance that India could develop in ways or act in ways that could affect the status of China or Japan, or the nature of the Sino-Japanese balance of power, would be a serious issue for a United Korea.

Two other, more hypothetical, situations also could significantly affect a United Korea's future. One is the possibility that the different subregions of Asia of which Korea is not part, namely, South Asia, Southeast Asia, and Central Asia, might learn a lesson from the countries that evolved into the European Union and attempt to create comparable subregional organizations. Such efforts would then raise questions about Northeast Asia pursuing such a model. Given Korea's relative size and power compared to the other members of such an entity—China and Japan—this option is unlikely to be deemed desirable by a United Korea. Fortunately for Korea, the chances of those other subregions emulating Europe are slim. If one or more of the subregions of Asia were to pursue that kind of vision, a United Korea and other smaller states in all of Asia would be well advised to try to get the advocates of any such plan to greatly expand the scope of their vision to include all of Asia. This would constitute the second hypothetical. Were there to be a pan-Asian version of the European Union, perhaps called the Asian Union, Koreans could contemplate a United Korea becoming one of its' member states in a federal or confederal structure, with the same degree of equanimity that a reunified Germany has displayed as a member of the European Union. While these situations are pointedly hypothetical, another option is more likely to become a factor for a United Korea on a regional basis.

While far from certain, there is a plausible chance that a number of states throughout Asia will organize themselves as a broadly defined economic free trade zone and/or as a collective security organization comparable to NATO. Were either to happen at the same time as the two Koreas were unifying, the future United Korea would simply incorporate each Korea's roles as part of the bargaining process. On the other hand, were either such organization to be created after a United Korea was established, Korean leaders would need to work assiduously with all the other budding members of the new organization to do their best to assure the organization is in Korea's national interests. How much success they would enjoy is anyone's guess, but regardless of how well they might do, after any such organization is in place it would be in the national interests of a United Korea to adapt to it as much as is feasible.

Moving beyond Asian regional issues, a United Korea also would have to address its global role. With the exception of one relatively minor loss that would be a certainty, namely, the fact that by creating one Korean nation-state as the legitimate government of Korea, the people of Korea would be giving up one of their two votes in the United Nations General Assembly, a United Korea would be unlikely to confront any negative factors on a global level of international relations. A United Korea's role at the United Nations could be influenced by the nature of its relations with permanent members of the UN Security Council. As explained above, both China and the United States—each serving on the Security Council—are likely candidates to have special relationships with a United Korea. If a United Korea were to have solid relations with both China and the United States, that would make its activities at the United Nations that much smoother. However, if a United Korea were to have solid relations with one at the expense of the other, that would tend to make U.S.-PRC interactions at the United Nations somewhat more strained with spillover effects on Korea. Beyond those two players on the UN stage, a United Korea also might be able to make use of Russia's stake in Korea via its Security Council role. Moreover, a United Korea might have to deal with Japan as a permanent member of the Security Council, if Tokyo ever realizes its ambitions to acquire that status. That turn of events could be a plus or a minus for a United Korea, depending upon Japan's perspective regarding Korean reunification, upon the nature of Sino-Japanese relations at that stage, and upon Japan's relations with the United States, should Korean reunification bring about an end to the U.S. strategic-buffer role for Japan-Korea relations. Clearly there would be a number of marginal uncertainties regarding a United Korea's global place at the United Nations.

Beyond those issues, a United Korea could also anticipate being looked to by a number of troubled countries around the world as a role model for them to use in resolving their internal disputes. A United Korea could be a passive role model—making the record of its reconciliation and reunification negotiations available to all who might learn from them. Alternatively, it could be an assertive role model—actively seeking to export its expertise on how to reduce tensions and build confidence. In a somewhat similar vein, to the extent a United Korea were to be the result of external mediation and assistance from one or more countries, Korea also could expect to be treated by the countries of the United Nations as an example of post-conflict nation-building worthy of emulation. Moreover, drawing on past ROK participation in United Nations Peace Keeping Operations (PKO), joint ROK-DPRK armed-forces units would likely serve in PKO roles for the United Nations as part of the inter-Korean confidence-building process, it is very likely that a United Korea would continue to use some of its armed forces in that manner. Given the heritage of a United Korea's PKO forces, they would present a particularly symbolic message on behalf of preserving peace.

Although it is a cliche, it remains true that only time would tell how well a United Korea would do internationally on regional and global levels. Korean leaders obviously should try to do their best in that regard, but there would be many independent variables over which they could exert little control. In that sense a United Korea would be in the same boat in uncertain waters as virtually all other countries. While that may not sound very optimistic, describing a United Korea's future status as being as normal as all those countries would in fact be very significant when compared to where its predecessor two Koreas had been for so many years. To be in that position would be a source of considerable pride for Koreans dwelling in a United Korea.

That level of pride about being a normal country with normal problems would be a major accomplishment. For Koreans in a United Korea their future would entail paying close attention to the same set of domestic and international political, economic, strategic, and diplomatic issues as any other independent nation-state. Citizens of any state know it may succeed or fail. Citizens of any state would live with the consequences. What would make a United Korea particularly attuned to the tasks before it would be its people's and its leaders' profound awareness of what had been overcome to create a United Korea. Against that background and with that motivation, the odds would seem to favor Korea staying on a proper domestic and international course that would permit it to succeed. After all, Korea as a once-divided nation would have far more incentive than most countries to pursue its *national* interests with a unique understanding of what it means to be a united nation in the United Nations.

Notes

CHAPTER 1: INTRODUCTION AND THE GEOGRAPHICAL SETTING

1. Those readers who want to keep up with current news on Korea are encouraged to use the following Internet Web sites: *Korea Times* (http://www.times.hankooki.com); *Korea Herald* (http://www.Koreaherald.co.kr); *Korea Economic Institute* (http://www.keia.com); and *Korean Central News Agency of DPRK* (http:/www.kcna.co.jp).

2. Korea's role as a regional vortex was carefully assessed in one of the best early treatments of Korean affairs: Gregory Henderson, *Korea: The Politics of the Vortex* (Cambridge: Harvard University Press, 1968).

3. For in-depth coverage of Korea's physical geography, see Shannon McCune, *Korea's Heritage: A Regional and Social Geography* (Rutland, VT and Tokyo: Charles E. Tuttle Co., 1956); and Organizing Committee of the 29th International Geographical Congress, *Korean Geography and Geographers* (Seoul: Hanul Academy, 2000).

CHAPTER 2: THE LEGACY OF ANTIQUITY

1. Readers interested in more in-depth treatments of Korean history should consider reading Woo-Keun Han, *The History of Korea* (Honolulu: University Press of Hawaii, 1980); Carter J. Eckert, Ki-baek Lee, Young

Ick Lew, Michael Robinson, and Edward W. Wagner, *Korea Old and New: A History* (Cambridge and Seoul: Korea Institute/Harvard University Press and Ilchokak Publishers, 1990); Kenneth B. Lee, *Korea and East Asia: The Story of a Phoenix* (Westport, CT: Praeger, 1997); and Bruce Cumings, *Korea's Place in the Sun: A Modern History* (New York: W.W. Norton, 1997).

2. For background on Korea's prehistoric roots and evolution into what became known as Korea, see Jeong-hak Kim, *The Prehistory of Korea* (Honolulu: University Press of Hawaii, 1979); and Hyung-il Pai, *Constructing "Korean" Origins: A Critical Review of Archeology, Historiography, and Racial Myths in Korean State-Formation Theories* (Cambridge: Harvard University Asia Center, 2000).

3. *Oxford English Dictionary*, online at http://dictionary.oed.com/.

4. For a Korean analysis of Paekche as the decisive external factor in the shaping of what would become Japan, see Wontack Hong, *Paekche of Korea and the Origin of Yamato Japan* (Seoul: Kudara International, 1994).

5. For basic background on the value systems (Buddhism, Confucianism, and Taoism) that spread from China to Korea and greatly influenced the latter's development, see Ninian Smart, *The World's Religions* (Englewood Cliffs, NJ: Prentice Hall, 1989).

6. For a concise overview of neo-Confucianism's development, beliefs, and impact, see H.G. Creel, *Chinese Thought from Confucius to Mao Tse-tung* (New York: Mentor Books, 1953).

7. The Western term "Manchurian" stems from a word "manchu" that the Khitan/Chin people subsequently applied to themselves, but it is used here because it is commonly applied to that region of Northeast Asia.

CHAPTER 3: THE IMPERIAL AGE

1. For insightful reviews of those relationships, see Dun J. Li, *The Ageless Chinese: A History* (New York: Charles Scribner's Sons, 1965); and Franz Michael, *China Through the Ages: History of a Civilization* (Boulder: Westview Press, 1986).

2. For a concise survey of those interactions, see Robert Collins, *East to Cathay: The Silk Road* (New York: McGraw-Hill, 1968).

3. The importance of the United States-Korea Inchon Treaty for Korea's international relations and for United States-Korea relations was commemorated on its centennial anniversary in 1982 in several scholarly works that also dealt with many of the awkward consequences that the 1882 agreement unleased. For example, see Han Sung-joo, ed., *After One Hun-*

dred Years: Continuity and Change in Korean-American Relations (Seoul: Asiatic Research Center, Korea University, 1982); Kwak Tae-hwan, et al., eds., *U.S.-Korean Relations, 1882–1982* (Seoul: Kyungnam University Press, 1982); and Ronald A. Morse, ed., *A Century of United States-Korean Relations* (Washington, D.C.: University Press of America, 1983). For additional background on the context in which United States-Korean relations began, see Martina Deuchler, *Confucian Gentlemen and Barbarian Envoys: The Opening of Korea, 1875–1885* (Seattle: University of Washington Press, 1977).

4. For an overview of the imperial system into which Korea was absorbed and became a core element, see Hilary Conroy, *The Japanese Seizure of Korea, 1868–1910* (Philadelphia: University of Pennsylvania Press, 1993); and Ramon H. Myers and Mark R. Peattie, eds., *The Japanese Colonial Empire, 1895–1945* (Princeton: Princeton University Press, 1984).

5. This slogan began with Rudyard Kipling's advocacy of imperialism as a means to uplift backward peoples through the spread of Western civilization in his "The White Man's Burden," *McClure's Magazine*, February 1899, but it became ammunition for Western critics of imperialist policies.

6. For a sense of that critical negativity, see the coverage of this period in the volume by Kenneth Lee, *Korea and East Asia*, 1997.

7. For insights into how that legacy influenced South Korea's economic successes, see Carter J. Eckert, *Offspring of Empire: The Koch'ang Kims and the Colonial Origins of Korean Capitalism, 1876–1945* (Seattle: University of Washington Press, 1991).

CHAPTER 4: LIBERATION AND DIVISION

1. The author focused on the long-term consequences of the "in due course" concept in *Toward Normalizing U.S.-Korea Relations: In Due Course?* (Boulder: Lynne Rienner Publishers, 2002).

2. Quoted in Lee Yur-bok, *West Goes East: Paul Georg von Mollendorff and Great Power Imperialism in Late Yi Korea* (Honolulu: University of Hawaii Press, 1988), p. 25.

3. For coverage of that sensitive period of U.S. relations with Korea, see E. Grant Meade, *American Military Government in Korea* (New York: King's Crown Press, 1951); and "The Gates of Chaos," in Gregory Henderson, *Korea: The Politics of the Vortex* (Cambridge: Harvard University Press, 1968).

CHAPTER 5: SOUTH KOREA'S EVOLUTION, 1948–2004

1. For a cross-section of these Korean War studies, readers are urged to consult Bruce Cumings, *The Origins of the Korean War* (Princeton: Princeton University Press, 1981); Rosemary Foot, *The Wrong War: American Policy and the Dimensions of the Korean Conflict, 1950–1953* (Ithaca: Cornell University Press, 1985); and William Struek, *The Korean War: An International History* (Princeton: Princeton University Press, 1995).

2. For an in-depth and lengthy (966 pages) scholarly treatment of this comparison, see Sung Chul Yang, *The North and South Korean Political Systems: A Comparative Analysis* (Seoul and Boulder: Seoul Press and Westview Press, 1994).

3. For in-depth insights into that era's details, see Sungjoo Han, *The Failure of Democracy in South Korea* (Berkeley: University of California Press, 1974).

4. For background on South Korea's foreign policy in its formative stages, see Byung Chul Koh, *The Foreign Policy Systems of North and South Korea* (Berkeley: University of California Press, 1984).

5. For coverage of the Koreagate scandal, see Robert Boettcher, *Gifts of Deceit, Sun Myung Moon, Tongsun Park, and the Korea Scandal* (New York: Holt, Rinehart and Winston, 1980); and William H. Gleysteen, Jr., *Massive Entanglement, Marginal Influence: Carter and Korea in Crisis* (Washington, D.C.: Brookings Institution, 1999).

CHAPTER 6: NORTH KOREA'S EVOLUTION, 1948–2004

1. For useful coverage of North Korea's development and its policies, see Young Whan Kihl, *Politics and Policies in Divided Korea: Regimes in Contest* (Boulder: Westview Press, 1984); Dae-sook Suh, *Kim Il Sung: A Biography* (Honolulu: University of Hawaii Press, 1989); Han S. Park, ed., *North Korea: Ideology, Politics, Economy* (Englewood Cliffs, NJ: Prentice Hall, 1996); and Bruce Cumings, *North Korea: Another Country* (New York: The New Press, 2004).

2. For background on that transition and its impact on North Korea, see Thomas H. Henriksen and Jongryn Mo, eds., *North Korea after Kim Il Sung: Continuity of Change?* (Stanford: Hoover Institution Press, 1997); and Dae-sook Suh and Chae-jin Lee, eds., *North Korea after Kim Il Sung* (Boulder: Lynne Rienner Publishers, 1998).

3. For background on North Korea's foreign policy in its formative stages, see Byung Chul Koh, *The Foreign Policy Systems of North and South Korea* (Berkeley: University of California Press, 1984).

CHAPTER 7: TWO KOREAS: INTERNATIONAL PERSPECTIVES

1. For major examples of earlier and recent examples of these dissenting American views, see Gregory Henderson, *Korea: The Politics of the Vortex* (Cambridge: Harvard University Press, 1968); Bruce Cumings, *The Two Koreas* (New York: Foreign Policy Association, 1984); Doug Bandow, *Tripwire; Korea and U.S. Foreign Policy in a Changed World* (Washington, D.C.: The Cato Institute, 1996); and Selig Harrison, *Korean Endgame; A Strategy for Reunification and U.S. Disengagement* (Princeton: Princeton University Press, 2002).

2. For insights into that era, see Chung Il-yung, ed., *Korea and Russia: Toward the 21st Century* (Seoul: The Sejong Institute, 1992); and Seung-ho Joo, *Gorbachev's Foreign Policy toward the Korean Peninsula, 1985–1991* (Lewiston, NY: Edwin Mellen Publisher, 2000).

3. For a comprehensive analysis of the Sino-Korean issue, see Chae-jin Lee, *China and Korea: Dynamic Relations* (Stanford: Hoover Institution Press, 1996).

4. For insights into that perspective, see Brian Bridges, *Japan and Korea in the 1990s: From Antagonism to Adjustment* (Aldershot: Edward Elgar Publishing, Ltd., 1993); and Victor Cha, *Alignment Despite Antagonism: The United States-Korea-Japan Security Triangle* (Stanford: Stanford University Press, 1999).

5. For a useful survey of Japan's efforts in that regard, see Yoshinori Kaseda, "Japan and the Korean Peace Process," in *The Korean Peace Process and the Four Powers*, eds. Tae-hwan Kwak and Seung-ho Joo (Aldershot: Ashgate Publishing, Ltd., 2003).

CHAPTER 8: REUNITING THE KOREAN NATION

1. For solid examples of such analyses, see Hakjoon Kim, *Unification Policies of South and North Korea: A Comparative Study* (Seoul: Seoul National University Press, 1978); Bong-youn Choy, *A History of the Korean Reunification Movement: Its Issues and Prospects* (Peoria, IL: Institute of International Studies, Bradley University, 1984); and B.C. Koh, "South Korea's Unification Policy" and Han Shik Park, "North Korea's Ideology and Unification Policy" in *The Prospects for Korean Reunification*, eds. Jay

Speakman and Chae-jin Lee (Claremont, CA: Keck Center, Claremont McKenna College, 1993).

2. The author questioned claims to such sincerity in two op-ed columns that proved to be controversial among policy advocates. See "Does Anyone Really Want Korean Reunification?" *Asian Wall Street Journal*, May 16, 1983; and "The Catch-22s of Korean Unification," *Asian Wall Street Journal*, June 1–2, 1984.

3. For detailed analyses of his policy, see Moon Chung-in and David I. Steinberg, eds., *Kim Dae-jung Government and Sunshine Policy: Promises and Challenges* (Washington, D.C. and Seoul: Georgetown University and Yonsei University Press, 1999).

4. For example, see Nicholas Eberstadt, *Korea Approaches Reunification* (Armonk: M.E. Sharpe, 1995); and Marcus Noland, *Avoiding the Apocalypse: The Future of the Two Koreas* (Washington, D.C.: Institute for International Economics, 2000).

5. The author explored the logic behind that concept in greater detail in his "A Korean Solution to the United States' Korean Problems," *Journal of East Asian Affairs* (Fall/Winter 2003).

6. Selig S. Harrison, *Korean Endgame: A Strategy for Reunification and U.S. Disengagement* (Princeton: Princeton University Press, 2002).

CHAPTER 9: CONCLUSION: UNITED KOREA'S PROSPECTS

1. For an example of what could cause such a change in the PRC, see Gordon G. Chang, *The Coming Collapse of China* (New York: Random House, 2001).

2. For insights into the virtues of Korean neutrality, see In-kwan Hwang, "Neutralization: An All-Weather Paradigm for Korean Reunification," *Asian Affairs: An American Review* (Winter 1999).

Index

About the Author

EDWARD A. OLSEN is Professor of National Security Affairs and Asian Studies at the U.S. Naval Postgraduate School in Monterey, California. Prior to joining the faculty there, he was a political analyst on Korea and Japan at the U.S. Department of State, Bureau of Intelligence and Research.